art / shop / eat

London

S0-BYW-521

Delia Gray-Durant

ten things to do

[1] View Westminster, the Thames and beyond from the slowly rotating London Eye (*pictured below and see p. 33*).

[2] Visit the British Museum (*see p. 69*): Egyptian mummies, Greek statues, Roman coins, Chinese vases; artefacts from pre-history to modern fascinatingly explained and displayed.

[3] Buy one of Ian Bennett's snappy hats in his boutique (*see p. 40*) on the South Bank; couture, cloth cap or baseball cap, you can get them all from the milliner of the millennium.

[4] Visit both iconic Tate galleries: Tate Modern (*see p. 27*) and Tate Britain (*see p. 101*). You can travel between the two on the Tate Boat (*see p. 8*) decorated by Damien Hirst.

[5] See the markets which have provided London with its food for hundreds of years: Smithfield (meat; *see p. 63*), Leadenhall (meat and fish; *see p. 61*), and Borough (fruit and veg; *see p. 40*).

[6] Study examples of Sir Christopher Wren's beautiful classical architecture at St Paul's Cathedral (*see p. 44*) and the Monument (*see p. 54*).

[7] Take tea in Claridges hotel (*see p. 12*), where the restored 1920s Art Deco interior features an ultra-modern Dale Chihuly chandelier.

[8] Identify 15 species of waterfowl in St James's Park (*see p. 109*), watch the feeding of the pelicans at 3pm, and take a guided tour of Duck Island.

[9] Stroll in Kensington Gardens (*map p. 120, C1–D2*) with its Princess Diana memorial fountain designed by Kathryn Gustafson.

[10] Have a cocktail with a view. Vertigo 42 in the City is the ultimate skyscraping London bar (*see p. 60*).

contents

About this guide

Vast and varied, London might seem daunting, but this book takes a unique approach to guiding visitors in a clear and concise way through the city, dividing it into five districts and providing the information you need for a great day out in any one of them: the South Bank, the City, Bloomsbury and the West End, Westminster and Kensington, each with its own distinctive character and major sites.

Within each section the major **art** collections are covered in depth, as well as other monuments and museums to visit **in the area**. Each section has suggestions on where to **eat**, and selected recommendations on where to **shop**.

Practicalities include a brief background to London, how to travel around, the latest on food, and a short selection of places to stay. The **history** provides the dates of key events, and the **glossary** at the end of the book explains certain art terms and gives information on major figures mentioned in the text. With the help of the **index** you can dip in and out of the book.

There are excellent **maps** throughout, inside the front cover is a map of all London, clearly indicating where the detailed maps to each district are to be found at the beginning of their sections. The numbers (**1**) on the maps locate the cafés and restaurants described later in that section, and the letters (**A**) locate the shops.

Enjoy London and do not hesitate to contact us with any views, recommendations or corrections: **www.artshopeat.com**

practicalities

INTRODUCTION

London is a multi-textured city, constantly vibrant and evolving, cosmopolitan yet uniquely royal with a deal of pomp and circumstance. The heartbeat of London is the river Thames, linking ancient and modern, from the London Eye to the Tower of London, and the Houses of Parliament to Shakespeare's Globe Theatre. Its lungs are the remarkable green public spaces at the very centre: Hyde Park, Green Park and St James's Park.

Culturally, London is second to none hosting seven of the top forty most-visited museums in the world in 2007. The great permanent collections in the British Museum, the National Gallery, the Victoria and Albert museum and the Tate museums, contain visual arts and antiquities of every type and every era, and are free of charge. Lesser-known museums, such as The Courtauld Gallery, the Wallace Collection and Sir John Soane's Museum, house superb collections in interesting buildings. There are numerous royal associations with London's ancient stronghold, the Tower of London, which contains the Crown Jewels, as well as with the two great churches, Westminster Abbey and St Paul's Cathedral. In the performing arts there is a wealth of choice, both in traditional and experimental music, theatre and dance. On the South Bank alone are three concert halls in the Southbank Centre, three theatres in the National Theatre, and the recently re-opened BFI Southbank film theatre.

When it comes to eating, London's restaurants are now in a class of their own and are constantly packed—the quality of food and cooking has become a serious occupation, both for the producer and the consumer. Whether you prefer to eat in starred restaurants or traditional pubs, in the museums or in the markets, British or International, the choice is yours.

GETTING THERE

London has five international **airports**: Heathrow (www.heathrowair-port.com); Gatwick (www.gatwickairport.com); Stansted (www.stanstedairport.com); Luton (www.london-luton.co.uk); and City (www.londoncityairport.com). Each of the airports have frequent train and bus services (and Underground services from Heathrow and City) to central London running from 5am to midnight. Full details are on each airport's website, and there are clear signs at the airports. The **Eurostar** train service operates from St Pancras station (*off map p. 67, A7*) to Paris and Brussels, and onward routes through Europe.

GETTING AROUND

A useful resource for planning your travels around London is www.tfl.gov.uk with an invaluable journey planner function and up-to-date information on route closures. By far the quickest way to get around London is by **Underground** (or Tube). Trains run frequently from 5.30am until midnight. The Underground system has been in constant use since 1860 and there is frequent ongoing engineering work. It tends to be very crowded during commuter rush hour (8–10am & 4–6pm) and some of the lines run deep underground, necessitating long escalators and tunnels. Nevertheless, travelling on the Underground is a rapid means of getting around London and a unique experience. **Buses** operate regularly from early morning to late in the evening with numerous night bus routes. The famous red Routemaster buses operate on routes 9 (Piccadilly Circus to Kensington) and 15 (Oxford Street to the City). It is

Travelling on the famous red Routemaster buses is one of the best unofficial tours of the city

a/s/e London

expensive to bring a **car** into the centre of London (car drivers must pay a congestion charge), traffic jams are a part of London life and hotel parking is limited. **Taxis,** also known as 'black cabs', can be hailed on the street. Alternatively you can use Telephone Taxi One: 0871 871 8710. Commuter **boat** services on the River Thames run between Embankment and Woolwich, Putney and Blackfriars, and Docklands. The 'Tate to Tate' ferry service is a useful link between the museums. The best **tickets** to use for travel over a few days are the Travelcard (for 1, 3 or 7 days) covering travel on the Underground, some overground trains, London buses and some river transport. These can be bought in newsagents or at any Underground station. The Oyster Card (electronic smart card) offers cheaper travel for a longer stay. Cards can be bought from all Underground stations, or in advance from www.visitlondon.com/travel.

VISITOR INFORMATION

The Britain and London Visitor Centre (BLVC) has a wealth of information that is useful for planning your time in the city. Its main office is at 1 Lower Regent Street (*map p. 67, C5*), open Mon–Fri 9.30–6.30, weekends and holidays 10–4, Underground: Piccadilly Circus. The official British tourism website www.visitbritain.com has a useful accommodation search facility as well as good links to the major sights in London.

ENTERTAINMENT

London has a wealth of entertainment, from world-class opera venues such as the Royal Opera House at Covent Garden to unique festivals such as the Lord Mayor's Show in November each year. For entertainment listings, London's daily newspaper, the Evening Standard, is an excellent source with a free supplement on Thursdays reviewing the latest in anything you would like to eat, see, buy and listen to in the city. Their online guide is www.thisislondon.co.uk. Try also www.viewlondon.co.uk.

SHOPS

In general shops open Monday to Saturday from around 9.30–6.30 (with longer opening hours on Oxford Street), and late-night shopping on Thursdays. The main shopping districts are Oxford Street (*map p. 66, B1-67, B5*) for the biggest choice of shops and department stores, Old and New Bond Street (*map p. 66, B3-66, C4*) for designer boutiques, and Knightsbridge (*map p. 121, E3*) for the luxury department stores Harrods and Harvey Nichols. There are fewer shops in the City and on the South Bank. London has a number of historic markets which are open from early morning and offer excellent shopping and eating opportunities. The best among them are Borough (*see p. 40*) for culinary delicacies, Brick Lane (*see p. 61*) for bric-a-brac, and Spitalfields (*see p. 63*) for original crafts.

FOOD & DRINK

London's reputation as a world centre of gastronomic excellence has swept the board in recent years and for Londoners eating-out has become a serious occupation. The trend for good cooking has been on an upturn since the 1980s. Celebrity chefs such as Gordon Ramsay, Rick Stein, Jamie Oliver, Hugh Fernley-Whittingstall and Raymond Blanc, have done much to encourage an interest in good eating. And not to be left out of the London restaurant bonanza, French chefs Joël Robuchon and Alain Ducasse have moved in.

Top-rate British-sourced ingredients, which have always been available, have finally gained recognition, such as Stilton and Cheddar cheeses, Welsh lamb, Scottish beef and salmon, Cornish crab, Yorkshire rhubarb and Hampshire watercress. Hand in hand with this is the increasing trend to select seasonal and organically-produced ingredients, and a renewed appreciation of age-old delicious vegetables such as beetroot, cabbage and parsnips, and a return to handmade traditional specialities such as raised meat pies and locally cured hams. The British cooking renaissance has touched long-established restaurants, and encouraged a new wave such as Roast (*see p. 38*) in Borough Market or St John (*pictured overleaf, and see p. 58*) at Smithfield.

But that is only half the story. The cosmopolitan character of London's restaurants goes back a long way, most noticeably to the period following the Second World War, when Italian, Greek, Russian, Jewish and Chinese restaurants appeared, particularly in Soho or the East End. Food from the Indian sub-continent has become so much a

London

a/s/e

St John restaurant and bakery, close to Smithfield meat market

part of the UK scene that curry now sits alongside fish and chips as a national dish. As more newcomers open high-quality restaurants the result is an increasing opportunity to eat every conceivable type of international food from Caribbean to Moroccan to Argentinian, and sample every imaginable dish from baba ganoush to brioche, or dim sum to haggis.

Eating in museum restaurants has become an integral part of the culture scene and England pioneered the concept: the first director of the V&A, Henry Cole, envisioned that the body should be nourished as well as the mind when visiting a museum. Since then the trend has roller-coastered. Museum restaurants now are not simply somewhere to stop off for a snack when your feet are aching, but serious and attractive places for a meal, patronised by museum visitors and local business people. Outstanding, but individual, are the restaurants at the National Portrait Gallery (*see p. 91*), the Royal Festival Hall (Skylon; *see p. 37*), Tate Britain (*see p. 114*), and the Wallace Collection (*see p. 91*).

Drink is taken just as seriously as food in London. Beer, considered a national institution and a 'democratic' drink, has traditionally contributed to the alcohol, energy and nutrient content of the British diet. London's alehouses go back a long way and there is evidence that beer, or mead, has been drunk in London for around 4,000 years. Originally flavoured with herbs and spices, the hop, now an essential component, was introduced in the 15th century. Beers, once locally brewed, developed distinctive characteristics, but by the mid-20th century, bland, processed beers swamped the market. In retaliation, in 1970 the term 'real ale' was championed to identify traditionally brewed beers with natural ingredients, which are matured in the cask to develop unique flavours and served using hand pulls. Pubs with the 'Good Beer' sign indicate a well-nurtured pint of real ale. Among them are the Anchor Bankside, Southwark; the Museum Tavern, Great Russell Street (*see p. 91*); and the Shepherds Tavern, Hertford Street (*see p. 115*). Pubs now vary greatly, from a traditional place to prop up the bar and have a good pint, to upmarket 'gastro' pubs serving classy food, and located in historical city gems.

In London, cocktail, champagne or wine bars are increasingly popular. English sparkling wines are starting to hold their own. The cool conditions and chalky soil of Sussex, on the south coast, are similar to Champagne's and the better English sparklings are made from Chardonnay, Pinot Noir and Pinot Meunier. Although not the same as AOC (Appellation d'Origine Contrôlée) Champagnes, some English vintages have held out well in blind tastings, notably Nyetimber Classic Cuvée (from Sussex), Chapel Down Pinot Reserve (from Kent) and Cuvée Merrett Cavendish from Ridge View (also Sussex). English wineries, notably in southeast and southwest England, are also producing respectable white wines.

Recommended restaurants are given in each section of this book. Our favourite restaurants carry the Blue Guides Recommended sign: ■ (see www.blueguides.com for more details). Categories are according to price per person for dinner, with wine:

££££	£100+
£££	£50–£100
££	£20–£50
£	under £20

WHERE TO STAY

With some 100,000 rooms available in London in every category, from B&Bs to top-class boutique hotels, there is an overwhelming choice. Rooms in the City are quiet at weekends but it's possible to get some very good rates; Soho, Piccadilly and Mayfair place you right in the thick of shopping and nightlife; Kensington and Knightsbridge offer some of the most elegant upmarket accommodation in the city, in gentrified surroundings.

In this section you will find only a selection of the accommodation available in London. Hotels that are particularly good (in terms of location, charm, value for money) carry the Blue Guides Recommended sign: ■ (see www.blueguides.com for more details). The prices below are a guideline for a double room in high season:

££££	£300+
£££	£200–£300
££	£100–£200
£	under £100

££££ Brown's Hotel, *Albermarle Street, Tel: 020 7493 6020, reservations 0870 460 8040, www.brownshotel.com, 117 rooms, Underground: Green Park. Map p. 97, B2*. Discreet, sophisticated and historic, Brown's was the first hotel to open in London 170 years ago. Taken over by the Rocco Forte Collection in 2003, it has conserved a classic and elegant English look. Top of the range suites overlook Dover and Albermarle Street, with an up-to-the-minute Spa. The Grill at Brown's (*Tel: 020 7493 6020*),

with tables draped in purest white linen, is the setting for breakfast, lunch and dinner, and there is live jazz (Mon–Fri, 9–midnight), and Brazilian Bosa Nova one night a month in the Donovan Bar.

££££ Claridge's, *Brook Street, Tel: 020 7629 8860, www.claridges.co.uk, 203 rooms and suites, Underground: Bond Street, Map p. 66, C2*. ■ Claridge's is a very special place, sophisticated and luxurious yet relaxed and unintimidating, with superb but discreet service. It was opened by Mr and Mrs

William Claridge in 1854 and was already patronised by royalty in 1860. Visits by Elizabeth II and Churchill are among several remembered in photographs in the lobby from where a staircase sweeps up to wide corridors. Each spacious room or suite is uniquely decorated, from opulent traditional to elegant art deco and restful modern, or a combination of all three. They include popular rooms designed by David, Lord Linley, the Queen's nephew. Public rooms include the Gordon Ramsay Restaurant at Claridge's; drinks are served in the Macanudo Fumoir and Claridge's Bar, and tea in the Foyer Room, graced with a Chihuly chandelier, and the Reading Room.

££££ London Marriott County Hall, *Westminster Bridge Road, Tel: 020 7928 5200, www.marriottcountyhall.com, 200 rooms, Underground: Waterloo. Map. p. 24, C2*. The Marriott is in a remarkable position on the banks of the river Thames looking towards Big Ben (*see p. 110*), with the London Eye (*see p. 33*) next door. The hotel occupies part of the monumental

The Lobby Bar at One Aldwych hotel

County Hall, formerly the Greater London Council's headquarters which opened in 1922. Inside, curved corridors follow the contours of the building, fine mirrors, fireplaces and carvings, and original panelling are offset by the deep reds and greens of the upholstery. The bar and restaurant overlook the Thames. All the bedrooms and suites are spacious and sumptuous, and several have river views, notably the Balcony Studios. There is a large Fitness Centre on the 6th floor with an excellent 25m pool, and a Health and Beauty Spa on the 5th floor.

£££££ One Aldwych, *1 Aldwych, Tel: 020 7300 1000, www.onealdwych.com, 105 rooms, Underground: Covent Garden, Temple. Map p. 67, C7.* ■ A modern hotel in a building of 1907, One Aldwych is an exercise in elegant understatement. The service is impeccable but not intimidating, every space contains works from the fabulous 350-piece collection of contemporary art, and beautiful flowers abound. Careful thought is given to small details in the bedrooms and bathroom: soft edges, luxury fabrics, restful colours, unobtrusive lighting. Every type of room is equally well presented. The swimming pool has underwater music, and there is a screening room. The Lobby Bar (*pictured above*) is a favourite rendezvous, as are both of its restaurants: Axis (*see p. 89*) and Indigo, overlooking the Lobby Bar.

£££ Dukes Hotel, *35–36 St James's Place, Tel: 020 7491 4840, www.dukeshotel.co.uk, 90 rooms, Underground: Green Park, Piccadilly Circus. Map p. 66, D4.* ■ This is heaven indeed, in a truly marvellous location on the doorstep of Green Park, St James's and Piccadilly. A total refurbishment completed in June 2007 improved the lighting and updated soft furnishings in the rooms. The hotel exudes calm and exclusivity in a low-key way. Less low-key are its famous martinis in the Duke's bar which is open to non-residents for light lunches. The dining room serves fine English dishes (Dressed Cornish crab, Loin of lamb), and in the elegant drawing room English tea is available (3–6pm). The health club has an Italian marble steam room.

£££ The Zetter, *86–88 Clerkenwell Road, Tel: 020 7324 4444, www.thezetter.com, 59 rooms, Underground: Farringdon. Map p. 42, A2.* This

N Оⁿoooooooooo

contemporary boutique hotel, overlooking St John's Square is convenient for Hatton Garden gold and silver district, and the City. The building has kept its 19th-century aura and the rooms, leading from a five-level atrium, feature stylish designer wallpapers and furnishings. The seven roof-top studios have patios. There is 24-hour room service and a special feature is the vending machines. Breakfast is served in the hotel's restaurant, The Zetter.

££ Durrants Hotel, *George Street, Tel: 020 7935 8131, www.durrantshotel.co.uk, 92 bedrooms, Underground: Bond Street. Map p. 66, B2.* In a prime position next to the shopping zone of Marylebone High Street, and close to the Wallace Collection (*see p. 82*), this is a welcoming hotel in a classic 18th-century building which conserves a period charm. Bedrooms are very comfortable without being over fussy, with good quality custom-made beds, and the bathrooms are marble clad. It has a restaurant and pleasant breakfast room, as well as a cosy bar, the George.

££ Georgian House Hotel, *35 St George's Drive, Tel: 020 7834 1438, www.georgianhouse hotel.co.uk, 53 rooms,*

Underground: Pimlico, Victoria. Map p. 96, G2. This charming family-run hotel, close to Victoria Station, occupies two vintage buildings in St George's Drive and Cambridge Street. Westminster, St James's Park (*see p. 109*) and Tate Britain (*see p. 101*) are within easy reach. Deluxe rooms include broadband internet connection, digital free-view TV, and DVD player and have particularly good showers. Standard rooms are not huge but nicely appointed, with compact showers or baths. In some rooms the original fittings are preserved. The Georgian House's 'basic rooms' (shared bathrooms and showers) on the 4th floor (no lift) are small but pretty. Excellent breakfast in room, no restaurant.

££ Hoxton Hotel, *81 Great Eastern Street, Tel: 020 7550 1000, www.hoxtonhotels.com, 204 rooms, Underground: Old Street. Map p. 42, A4.* ■ This purpose-built hotel, which opened in 2006, is backed by Pret-a-Manger co-founder, Sinclair Beecham. A novel and unpretentious establishment, it incorporates a number of simple but effective ideas, not the least of which is its internet-only special offers. All rooms are contemporary minimalist twins or doubles, with flat-screen TV, good showers and cosy duvets. A snack breakfast in a bag is included but full English is available in the Hoxton Grill. In a lively part of the City near to Spitalfields Market (*see p. 63*), with numerous bars and galleries in the vicinity, it's a fun place to stay.

££ Mayflower Hotel, *26 Trebovir Road, Tel: 020 7370 0991, www.mayflowerhotel.co.uk, 48 rooms, Underground: Earl's Court. Off map p. 121, G1.* ■ Inexpensive yet remarkably distinctive and sleek, this townhouse hotel is west of the South Kensington museums, next to Earl's Court Tube station. Presented in an original manner, it combines oak, walnut and marble floors with stainless steel modernity and exotic touches such as carved headboards, room fans, and richly coloured fabrics. All the rooms are individually designed. There is a refreshing juice-bar lounge, a bright, modern breakfast room, and a tiny tropical garden. Earl's Court has come a long way. No restaurant.

£ Celtic Hotel, *62 Guilford Street, Tel: 020 7837 6737, 35 rooms, Underground: Holborn, Russell Square. Map p. 67, A6.* The position, very close to Russell

A luxury double room at the Mayflower Hotel

Square, is remarkably quiet but the British Museum (*see p. 69*) is just a stone's throw away. It's convenient for the West End and on a direct Underground link to Heathrow. The hotel occupies a section of a Georgian terrace with a tiny garden. The pretty breakfast room runs the width of the building. The rooms (undergoing refurbishment) are no frills affairs, but comfortable, well kept, a relatively good size, and all have a hand-wash basin, but showers and toilets are shared. No restaurant.

£ Premier Inn County Hall, *Belvedere Road, Tel: 0870 238 3300, www.premierinn.com, 314 rooms, Underground: Waterloo. Map p. 24, C2.* In the same building as the Marriott County Hall (*see p. 13*) and in a superb position, but without the views, the breakfast room looks out towards the London Eye (*see p. 33*). The Premier Inn group offers economical deals. The modern bedrooms and bathrooms are simple with a variety of breakfast options.

£ Premier Inn Southwark, *34 Park Street, Tel: 0870 990 6402, 59 rooms, Underground: Borough, Southwark. Map p. 25, B5.* On the Thames at Bankside, in a prime position for exploring this part of London, the Premier Inn Southwark is tucked away behind the Anchor pub, in a lively area very close to Shakespeare's Globe Theatre (*see p. 35*) and Tate Modern (*see p. 27*). The rooms have recently been refurbished.

£ 22 York Street B&B, *22–24 York Street, Tel: 0207 224 2990, www.22yorkstreet.co.uk, 10 rooms, Underground: Baker Street. Map p. 66, A1.* This B&B is a home from home, and appeals to younger people. Continental breakfast is served in the kitchen at a large, communal table. There is nothing fancy about the rooms but they are light and airy, with wooden floors and French furniture; each has its own bathroom, TV, direct dial phone and hairdryer. The sitting room has tea and coffee-making facilities.

£ YHA London Central, *104–108 Bolsover Street, Tel: 0870 770 6144, www.yha.org.uk, 59 rooms, Underground: Great Portland Street, Regents Park. Map p. 66, A3.* Youth hostels have certainly shunned their image of a decade ago. The latest in high-tech, low-cost accommodation via the Youth Hostel Association has just opened in the heart of the West End. If you are travelling as a group or don't mind sharing a room (en-suite), then you can't get a better offer, and be closer to all the shopping, eating and major sights of London.

a/s/e London

history

Roman Era

43 AD The Romans occupy the north bank of the Thames and call their port Londinium. They build the first wooden bridge across the Thames. Despite raids by the Iceni led by Queen Boudicca, by c.190–200 London is an important Roman Imperial fortified outpost with some 40,000 inhabitants

Saxon Period

c. 441 Saxons dominate Britain, and by 672 Ludenwic (present area of Covent Garden; *map p. 67, C6*) is a thriving market town
886 King Alfred retaliates against waves of Danish invasion
1013 London capitulates to the Danes and King Canute makes London the capital in place of Winchester
c. 1045 The Palace of West Minster, built by Edward the Confessor, becomes seat of royal government

Normans and Plantagenets

1066 William the Conqueror crowns himself king in Westminster and orders the building of the White Tower; the foundation of the Tower of London fortress (*see p. 49*)
1176 The first London Bridge in stone replaces a succession of wooden ones
1193 The City of London has its first Lord Mayor, Henry Fitz-Ailwin
1220 Southwark Cathedral (*see p. 36*) construction begins
1245 The construction of the present Westminster Abbey (*see p. 105*) is begun under Henry III

Houses of Lancaster and York

1338 Under Edward III the Palace of Westminster becomes the meeting place of parliament
1348 The Black Death halves the city's population to 30,000

1397 Richard 'Dick' Whittington is elected Lord Mayor for the first of four times

1400–1500 Trader's guilds are established and London becomes a major European port

1483 Murder of the Princes in the Tower during the Wars of the Roses 1455–87, allowing their uncle, Richard III, to become King

The Tudors

1536–39 Dissolution of the monasteries during the Reformation under Henry VIII

1599 Shakespeare's plays appear on stage at The Globe theatre in Southwark; in 1997 the Globe (*see p. 35*) is reconstructed near its original site

1600 Wealthy land-owning families build mansions in the 'West End' of the capital

The Stuarts

1603 Elizabeth I, the last Tudor, dies

1605 The 'Gunpowder Plot' led by Guy Fawkes attempts to blow up parliament and the king (James I, and VI of Scotland)

1649 Charles I is executed and a Commonwealth is declared by Oliver Cromwell who rules England as a republic

1660 Restoration of the monarchy under Charles II

1665 The Great Plague of London kills up to 60,000 and wealthy families flee the city

1666 The Great Fire of London starts in Pudding Lane; the devastation it causes prompts Charles II to form a Rebuilding Commission. Under the direction of Sir Christopher Wren, 51 churches (*see p. 56*) and St Paul's Cathedral (*see p. 44*) are built, along with the reconstruction of the rest of the City area

Hanoverian and Georgian London

1701 Under William and Mary, Britain is the first country to have a constitutional monarchy

1746 Samuel Johnson signs a contract with publisher William Strahan at the Golden Anchor Tavern in Borough (*map p. 25, B6*) to produce a dictionary of the English language

a/s/e London

1753 The first collection of the British Museum (*see p. 69*) opens to the public, with important artefacts such as the Rosetta Stone and the Elgin Marbles arriving in the next two decades

1769 The Royal Academy (*see p. 110*) shows its first Summer Exhibition under the directorship of Joshua Reynolds

1788 Bank of England (founded 1694) moves into the Soane-designed building (of which only the curtain wall remains today)

1801 London's population reaches one million

1807 First street lighting introduced in Pall Mall (*map p. 97, C3*)

1825 John Nash transforms Buckingham House into a royal palace (*see p. 99*) intended for George IV; Queen Victoria is the first to live here

1829 Robert Peel establishes the Metropolitan Police Force

Victorian London

1837–39 Charles Dickens' *Oliver Twist* is serialised, exposing London's chronic poverty, health and education problems

1842 Queen Victoria makes her first train journey arriving at Paddington Station

1851 The Great Exhibition is held in the metal and glass Crystal Palace in Hyde Park (*see p. 130*), designed by Joseph Paxton

1863 The Metropolitan Line is the world's first underground railway

1883 The first public displays of electric light are conducted. Edison constructs the first power station at 57 Holborn Viaduct

1888 The London County Council (LCC) is created. The first legal strikes take place

1897 Henry Tate presents his art collection to the public in the building designed by Sidney Smith that will become Tate Britain (*see p. 101*)

1899 Queen Victoria lays the foundation stone of the Victoria and Albert Museum (*see p. 123*)

Descendants of Victoria and the House of Windsor

1914–18 First World War; 1915 Zeppelin raids over London

1922 The BBC starts broadcasting programmes from central London

1928 Women granted the vote following the efforts of the Suffragette movement

1939-45 Second World War; City and East End severely damaged in the Blitz.

1940 Winston Churchill becomes Prime Minister (*see p. 109*)

1951 Festival of Britain; post-war London shows off its architectural innovation by constructing the Royal Festival Hall (*see p. 31*) on the South Bank

1952 Elizabeth II crowned in Westminster Abbey (*see p. 105*)

1955 Heathrow airport opens

1960–68 The Swinging Sixties, London becomes a leader in music and fashion

1967 The 19th-century London Bridge is sold to an American buyer

1974 The wholesale fruit and vegetable market moves out of Covent Garden; the old buildings are saved and rejuvenated (*see p. 94*)

1994 Eurostar trains run between London and Paris and Brussels

2000 London votes for its first elected mayor, Ken Livingstone. As part of the new century's celebrations in the city, the Millennium Bridge (*see p. 34*) opens (and closes again temporarily), Tate Modern (*see p. 27*) shows its art in the former Bankside Power Station, and the 135m-high London Eye (*see p. 33*) takes its first paying customers, having been towed down the River Thames on barges before being winched into place on the South Bank

2002 The Queen's Golden Jubilee Celebrations

2005 London wins the bid for the 2012 Olympics; four terrorist bombings the next day shock London

2008 Heathrow's Terminal 5 opens

English Monarchs since 1066

House of Normandy
William I (The Conqueror) 1066–87
William II 1087–1100
Henry I 1100–35
Stephen 1135–54

House of Angevin
Henry II 1154–89
Richard I 1189–99
John 1199–1216

House of Plantagenet
Henry III 1216–72
Edward I 1272–1307
Edward II 1307–27
Edward III 1327–77
Richard II 1377–99

House of Lancaster
Henry IV 1399–1413
Henry V 1413–22
Henry VI 1422–61

House of York
Edward IV 1461–70
Edward V Apr–June 1483
Richard III 1483–85

House of Tudor
Henry VII 1485–1509
Henry VIII 1509–47
Edward VI 1547–53

House of Tudor contd.
Mary I 1553–58
Elizabeth I 1558–1603

House of Stuart
James I (VI Scotland) 1603–25
Charles I 1625–49
Charles II 1649–85
James II 1685–88
William III and Mary II 1689–1702 and 1689–94
Anne 1702–14

House of Hanover
George I 1714–27
George II 1727–60
George III 1760–1820
George IV 1820–30
William IV 1830–37
Victoria 1837–1901

House of Saxe-Coburg & Gotha
Edward VII 1901–10
George V 1910–36 (renamed House of Windsor in 1917)

House of Windsor
Edward VIII 1936
George VI 1936–52
Elizabeth II 1952–present

THE SOUTH BANK

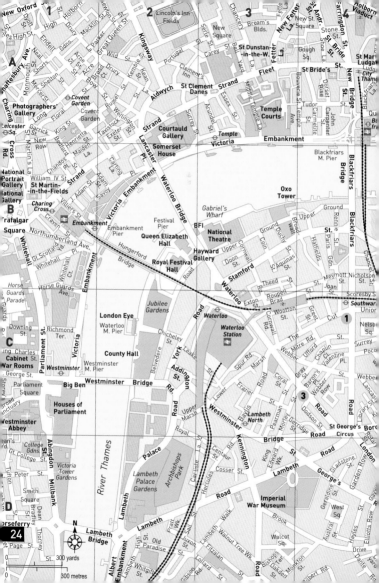

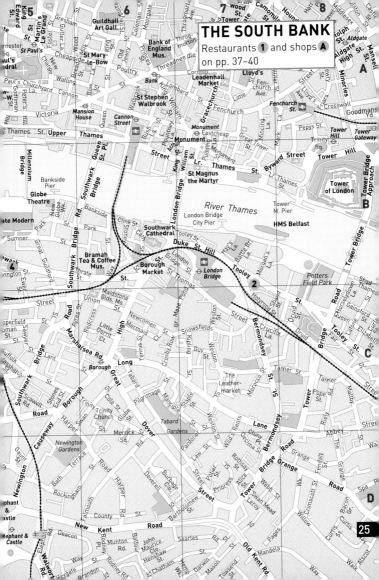

THE SOUTH BANK
Restaurants **1** and shops **A**
on pp. 37–40

introduction

A lively stretch of Thames riverside between Westminster Bridge and Tower Bridge, the South Bank is uninterrupted by traffic, rejuvenated and revived. It combines a riverside stroll and wonderful Thames vistas with some of the most important centres for the performing and visual arts in London.

The first bridge linking the north and south banks was constructed by the Romans close to the present London Bridge and consequently the area around it, Bankside and Southwark, has had a long and varied history: the proliferation of 16th century popular theatres; 18th century docks and warehouses; and 20th century cultural rejuvenation. The gothic Southwark Cathedral sits alongside the showcase contemporary engineering of the Millennium Bridge and the positively futuristic Southwark Underground station; the reconstruction of Shakespeare's Globe Theatre is towered over by the renovated power station that is now Tate Modern; and the striking Southbank Centre complex has been refurbished and remains the area's important cultural focus, conceived nearly 60 years ago during the post-war Festival of Britain.

Eating options in this part of London match the diversity of the cultural experiences on offer; many of the art institutions have their own cafés and restaurants. The riverside offers many dining rooms with views across the Thames. For shopping, there is the formidable Borough Market for every kind of British (and international) delicacy, and the boutiques at Oxo Tower Wharf for an eclectic browse.

Tate Modern

Open: Sun–Thur 10–6, Fri–Sat 10–10; closed 24–26 Dec
Charges: Free entry except special exhibitions **Tel:** 020 7887 8888
Web: www.tate.org.uk **Underground:** Blackfriars, Southwark
Boat: Every 40 minutes between Tate Modern & Tate Britain
Map: p. 25, B5
Highlights: *Seagram Murals* by Mark Rothko; *The Snail* by Matisse; *The Three Dancers* by Picasso; *The Uncertainty of the Poet* by Giorgio de Chirico

Since its opening in 2000, Tate Modern has become one of the most visited museums of modern art worldwide. It holds the national collection of British and international modern art from 1900 and resides in the transformed Bankside Power Station, a severe brick building designed by Giles Gilbert Scott to provide London's electricity after the Second World War. At the core of this unusual setting is the vast Turbine Hall, 35m high and 152m long, with a ramped access, providing space for colossal exhibits which have included Louise Bourgeois's *Giant Spider* in 2000 and Doris Salcedo's *Shibboleth* in 2007-08. The permanent collection is displayed on Levels 3 and 5, and there are regular special exhibitions.

Permanent collection

Tate Modern's approach to presenting their permanent collection is challenging and novel. Works are selected on a rotational basis and exhibited in a broadly thematic manner around four permanent central themes. The themes, based on pivotal movements, are Surrealism, Minimalism, Post-war Innovations in Abstraction and Figuration, and the links between Cubism, Futurism and Vorticism. The starting point of each section is a central 'hub' and works in the neighbouring galleries are chosen to set up dialogues between past and present by revealing historic precedents, evolutionary developments, opposing reactions, and long-term effects. The work of certain artists may correspond to more than one theme, and some galleries are devoted to a single artist.

27

London

a/s/e

Level 3, Poetry and Dream, Surrealism and Beyond: Drawing on Tate Modern's large and important collection of Surrealist works, this section brings together artists who were touched by, or reacted against, the Surrealist movement, launched in Paris in 1924 by the French poet André Breton. The dream-like and mysterious juxtapositions in Giorgio de Chirico's *The Uncertainty of the Poet* (1913) of a bunch of bananas and an antique torso placed in a piazza, served as a precedent to Surrealism. Surrealism's energy was harnessed by artists worldwide, to express the anguish of conflict or create hybrid figures: Joan Miró (*Women and Bird in the Moonlight*; 1949); Germaine Richier (*Water*; 1953–54); Matta (*Black Virtue*; 1943); and Constant (*After Us, Liberty*; 1949). Brilliant painter and writer Max Ernst, who attacked established cultural convention, wholeheartedly embraced Dada and Surrealism (*Celebes*; 1921), while Paul Klee, Edward Wadsworth and Alexander Calder explored the irrational and the unconscious. Picasso and Francis Bacon were both inspired to reinterpret the human figure. Picasso's *The Three Dancers* (1925) is the artist's interpretation of a triangular love affair with each figure seemingly caught in uncontrolled ferment. Other threads lead to the organic sculptures of Joseph Beuys which proved to be a pioneering influence on performance art, and the physical engagement of Cy Twombly's *Quattro Stagioni* series of paintings (1993–94). The counterpoint was the fiercely figurative work of Max Beckmann (*Carnival*; 1920), Stanley Spencer (*The Centurion's Servant*; 1914), Balthus (*Sleeping Girl*; 1943), and Meredith Frampton (*Portrait of a Young Woman*; 1945).

Level 3, Material Gestures: Painting and sculpture of the 1940s and 1950s illustrate new forms of abstraction and expressive figuration emerging in postwar Europe and America in a search to reveal inner worlds or universal truths. Barnett Newman's *Adam* (1951–52) and Anish Kapoor's *Ishi's Light* (2003) are a half-century apart but their strips or columns of light reveal similar affinities for exploring these universal truths. Soulages's *Painting 23 May, 1953* has a calligraphic quality, and sculptures by David Smith assemble familiar objects, such as farming tools (*Agricola VIII*; 1952). Mark Rothko's contemplative **Seagram Murals** (1959), a subdued maroon series, was originally commissioned for the restaurant in the Seagram Building in New York. Their oppressive nature was not felt to be appropriate for a restaurant setting and Rothko donated the series of nine paintings to the Tate instead. Matisse, Braque, Picasso and Miró were revolutionary abstractionists at the beginning and revered grand old men later in their careers. Matisse's **The Snail** (1953) was one of his largest pieces of cut-out with which he explored essential form and colour. A move away from abstraction was made by members of the Young British Art Movement in the 1990s. The movement is highlighted by Fiona Rae's *Night Vision* (1998) and Marlene Dumas's *Stern* (2004), which show a return to figuration and experimentation with the properties of paint. Spontaneous or by intent, the sensory nature of Abstract Expressionism is evoked by Monet's *Water-Lilies* (after 1916) and works by Jackson Pollock (*Summertime: Number 9A*; 1948).

Level 5, States of Flux: Cubism, Futurism, and Vorticism challenged the established norms of image making with a fractured evocation of the modern world in the first decades of the 20th century. Picasso in his early years of Cubism reached almost total abstraction using small facets and interacting planes of colour to make up his subjects, such as in his *Seated Nude* (1909–10). Umberto Boccioni's bronze, *Unique Forms of Continuity in Space* (1913) is a Futurist work, embracing the new industrialisation of Italy. Cubist collages and assemblages were reinvented by Pop artists of the 1960s consumer era, notably Eduardo Paolozzi in Britain with his series *Ten Collages from BUNK* (1948). From the States, Pop works range from Andy Warhol's *Marilyn Diptych* (1962), Roy Lichtenstein's *Whaam!* (1963) and *0 Through 9* (1961) by Jasper Johns, through to soft sculptures by Claes Oldenburg. In the film genre, Pop and Fluxus influenced the film diary of Jonas Mekas (*Diaries, Notes & Sketches a.k.a. Walden*; 1964–69) as well as British artist Steve McQueen's *Drumroll* (1998), a film triptych of city sounds and images. In

a/s/e London

contradistinction are post-Impressionist paintings by Gustave Klimt (*Portrait of Hermine Gallia*; 1904) and Pierre Bonnard (*The Window*; 1925), whose decorative use of colour was deeply intense.

Level 5, Idea and Object:

Minimalism of the 1960s was the impersonal and objective antidote to Expressionism and the search for an harmonious combination of scientific and spiritual ideas leading to a more perfect society. Works such as Kandinsky's *Swinging* (1925), Piet Mondrian's *Composition C* (1935), Naum Gabo's constructions (*Red Cavern*; c. 1926), Ben Nicholson's white reliefs (1934–36), and elegantly pared down sculptures by Constantin Brancusi (*Fish*; 1926) and Barbara Hepworth (*Forms in Echelon*; 1938), have similar objectives. Later came Carl André's brick 'sculpture' *Equivalent VIII* (1966) and Robert Mangold's *Red Wall* (1965). Sol LeWitt's sombre, impersonal floor to ceiling drawings, *Six Geometric Figures (+ Two) (Wall Drawings)* (1980-81), contrast with mass-produced strips of fluorescent lighting which Dan Flavin transforms into iconic objects (*The Diagonal of May 25, 1963*). Ellsworth Kelly painted hard-edged abstractions that are at times rooted in the visual world, such as *Broadway* (1958). Marcel Duchamp's urinal, *Fountain* (1917) invented the concept of the 'Readymade'–everyday manufactured objects endowed with a title by the artist. The Readymade was uniquely approached by the sculptor Joseph Beuys throughout his career: *The Pack* (1969), 24 sledges packed with emergency supplies, depicts the artist's memory of his plane crash during the Second World War and being rescued. Inner and outer worlds are explored in Cristina Iglesias's beautiful panels of woven metal strips, *Pavilion Suspended in a Room* (2005).

Tate Modern has plenty of opportunities for refreshment during or after a trip around the gallery. There is a fine restaurant and bar on Level 7 (*see p. 38*) with wonderful views across the Thames, an espresso bar on Level 4, and a café on Level 2. The large shop is on Levels 1 and 2.

Southbank Centre

Open: Royal Festival Hall foyer daily 10–10; Hayward Gallery
Sun–Thur 10–6, Fri–Sat 10–10; Queen Elizabeth Hall foyer daily
10–10; Saison Poetry Library Thur–Sun 10–8 **Charges:** Free entry
except for events, performances and exhibitions **Tel:** 0871 633 2500
Web: www.southbankcentre.org.uk **Underground:** Embankment,
Waterloo **Map:** p. 24, B2
Highlights: Royal Festival Hall auditorium; Saison poetry collection

Southbank Centre is London's premier arts complex, successfully
combining the performing arts, visual arts and literature. Regular cultural events revolve around three major buildings: the Royal Festival
Hall; the Queen Elizabeth Hall; and the Hayward Gallery.

The building of the Southbank Centre marked a transformation for
this section of the river from industrial to cultural. Begun in 1951 as
part of the Festival of Britain, its purpose was to revive the nation following the Second World War, and act as a showcase for exciting
contemporary architecture and innovative technology. The surround-
ing area was further developed in the 1970s to accommodate the
National Theatre, BFI Southbank (national film theatre) and the
Jubilee Gardens (created in 1977 to mark the Queen's Silver Jubilee).
The buildings and their austere concrete façades, particularly the
Hayward Gallery, have not won a place in the affections of many
Londoners, however, much money and effort has gone into renovating
the area in the last few years resulting in an exciting cultural district.

The **Royal Festival Hall** is the major concert hall of the complex, and
the only surviving building from the Festival of Britain construction.
Behind its curved façade, is a range of spaces for exhibitions and
events (many of them free) and a new glass lift glides up through the
six levels. The **auditorium** (*pictured overleaf*), suspended inside the
main structure—something like an Easter egg inside its box, according
to its architects—was always a successful concept, but its original
acoustics have been greatly enhanced with mechanically adjustable
sound absorbing fabrics and canopies or wings over the stage. The

31

a/s/e London

The Royal Festival Hall auditorium, newly renovated using the latest acoustic technology and decorated in its original Modernist style

original Modernist décor is still in place but the wooden stage has been reconfigured and divided into 11 individually controllable sections. The carpet pattern represents sound seen through an oscilloscope, the foyer walls have been returned to their strong 1950s Modernist colours, and the balustrades have been refurbished in postwar materials of bronze, copper and aluminium. This building also holds the **Saison Poetry Library** on Level 5 which has the most comprehensive and accessible collection of modern poetry in Britain.

The **Hayward Gallery** is a purpose-built temporary exhibition space in Brutalist 60s style, using quantities of shuttered concrete. It displays the work of 20th century and contemporary artists, sculptors and photographers, and organises the British Art Show which promotes significant emerging British artists. The gallery can be picked out at night by its Neon Tower (1970–72) of fluorescent tubes activated by the wind.

The **Queen Elizabeth Hall** is the second largest concert venue on the South Bank and hosts chamber concerts, choir, dance and opera.

London Eye

Open: Daily June–Sept 10–9, Oct–May 10–8; closed 25 Dec & mid-Jan (for annual maintenance) **Charges:** Entry charge; ticket office located in County Hall behind the Eye, or pre-booking service online **Tel:** 0870 5000 600 **Web:** www.londoneye.co.uk
Underground: Waterloo, Westminster **Map:** p. 24, C2

The London Eye, designed to commemorate the millennium, has become one of the most popular visitor attractions in the UK. The gently revolving wheel from which passenger capsules are suspended was initially criticised as a modern eyesore on the central London skyline, but now it is so familiar that attitudes have softened. The great steel circle stands between the old County Hall and the river Thames, and obscures neither buildings nor sky.

This massive yet satisfying structure was designed by husband and wife team, David Marks and Julia Barfield. Technologically innovative, 135m high with a circumference of 424m, it can carry 800 passengers in the 32 transparent capsules in each 30-minute revolution. The London Eye is essentially the same design as a bicycle wheel with a spindle holding the wheel structure and a hub revolving around the spindle. It took seven years to build and had to be transported up the Thames by barge in sections and assembled on site before being winched into place (which took a week) onto its 33m-deep steel and concrete foundations.

The Eye draws an amazing 3.5 million visitors a year and is a captivating experience that most vertigo sufferers can cope with. The speed of travel is almost imperceptible, and from the floating capsules are spectacular views of London. Landmarks that come immediately in view along the Thames are the Houses of Parliament and Big Ben (*see p. 110*), the Oxo Tower (*see p. 40*), Tower Bridge (*see p. 53*), and Canary Wharf, further to the east. Easy to spot is Buckingham Palace (*see p. 99*) in its gardens and, on a really good day, you might glimpse the Queen's other residence at Windsor, 25 miles away.

HMS Belfast (*open daily March–Oct 10–6, Nov–Feb 10–5, entry charge, Web: www.iwm.org.uk, Underground: London Bridge*). Moored on the banks of the river Thames, HMS Belfast is the last surviving Second World War armoured warship in Europe and makes for a unique museum. Built in Belfast and launched on 17th March 1938, she has an impressive war record, participating at the D-day landings in 1944, and being deployed during the Korean War (1950–53). The nine decks are fascinating to explore and a testament to the conditions in which the crew worked and lived. Above decks, highlights include the Admiral's bridge, compass platform and 6-inch gun turret. Below are the living quarters, mess decks and engine room. While negotiating the multitude of narrow ladders you may come across the two ship's cats. **Map p. 25, B8**

Imperial War Museum (*open daily 10–6, free entry, Web: www.iwm. org.uk, Underground: Lambeth North*). The city's foremost presentation of wartime experiences from the start of the First World War in August 1914 up to the present day. Since 1936, the Imperial War Museum has occupied the main building of the former Bethlem Royal Hospital for the insane; the dome (1846) is by Sidney Smith, the designer of Tate Britain (*see p. 101*). Over six floors, the displays use a remarkable range of presentations: memorabilia, fine art, film, sound archives, interactive audio-visuals, models, reconstructions and paintings to illustrate all aspects of warfare. The Large Exhibits Gallery, rising through the full height of the building, spectacularly displays large war machines suspended in space, including aircraft and a V2 Rocket. The museum's impressive collection of some 4,000 works of art commissioned during the First World War shows works by Paul Nash and Stanley Spencer. John Singer Sargent's monumental *Gassed* (1919) is permanently displayed. **Map p. 24, D3**

Millennium Bridge (*Underground: Blackfriars, Southwark*). The slender, steel suspension bridge spans the Thames between Tate Modern (*see p. 27*) on the south bank, and below St Paul's Cathedral (*see p. 44*) on the north bank. The winning design, by architect Norman Foster and sculptor Anthony Caro, is described as a 'blade of light' as it maintains a shallow profile in order to enhance the view of St Paul's (the supporting cables are below the deck). It was the first new river bridge in London since Tower Bridge in 1894, and the first ever exclusively for pedestrians. The bridge opened to great fanfare on 10th June 2000, and huge queues formed to make the first crossing. Almost immediately it was forced to close because the number of people, up to 2,000, caused the bridge to sway unsafely. The problem was finally rectified, at great expense, and the bridge reopened in February 2002. **Map p. 25, B5**

Shakespeare's Globe Theatre (*plays performed daily May–Sept, exhibition & tour open daily mid-May to mid-Sept 9–12.30 & 1–5, mid-Oct to mid-April 10–5, entry charge, Web: www.shakespeares-globe.org, Tel: 020 7902 1400, Underground: Blackfriars, Southwark*). Shakespeare's Globe is undoubtedly the most anomalous sight in London: a timber-framed, lathe and plaster, reed thatched, 20-sided polygon, dwarfed by the old power station home of the Tate Modern (*see p. 27*). Completed in 1997, it stands close to the site of the original Globe of 1599. Plays are performed exclusively in summer as the building is partly open to the sky—and to the noise of passing aircraft. Groundlings stand around the stage, other spectators sit on backless benches. The new theatre's design is as authentic as archaeological research allowed: English oak is used throughout and it

Detail of the striking entrance gates to Shakespeare's Globe Theatre

was assembled using traditional mortice and tenon joints and wooden pegs. An exhibition centre presents a colourful journey through Shakespeare's life and times. The elegant wrought-iron entrance gates illustrate quotations from Shakespeare's works (*pictured on previous page*). **Map p. 25, B5**

Southwark Cathedral (*London Bridge, open daily 8.30–5.30, free entry, Underground: London Bridge*). London's earliest example of Gothic architecture was begun in 1220; the upper parts of the tower are 14th–15th century and the pinnacles date from 1689. Fragments of earlier churches in the west-nave include a Norman door arch (1106), Gothic arcading, and two 15th-century wooden carved roof bosses, and in the south choir aisle is a section of Roman paving. The memorial to Shakespeare (*pictured below*) in the south aisle was erected in 1954, and a stained glass window above presents characters from his plays; alongside is a tablet to Sam Wanamaker, the American actor who was the driving force behind the new Globe theatre (*see p. 35 above*). In the north choir aisle, the Nonesuch Chest, a particularly beautiful piece of furniture for storing church records, was given to the cathedral in 1588. Shakespeare's brother was buried in the cathedral and a stone commemorates him in the choir. **Map p. 25, B6**

The memorial to William Shakespeare inside Southwark Cathedral

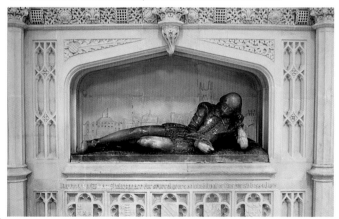

eat

Part of a day out on and around the South Bank is the choice of places to eat. The main cultural venues are well equipped to boost flagging attention spans, including Skylon at the Royal Festival Hall, and the restaurant at Tate Modern. Borough Market sells the raw materials and there are a host of cafés and restaurants at Jubilee Gardens next to the London Eye. Pubs, old and new, proliferate in this historically sociable part of London. For price categories, see p. 11; all restaurants are located on map pp. 24 & 25.

£££ Oxo Tower Restaurant, *OXO Tower Wharf (**map p. 24, B3**), Tel: 020 7803 3888, restaurant open Mon–Sat 12–2.30 & 6–11; Sun 12–3 & 6.30–10; brasserie open Mon–Sat 12–3 & 5.30–11; Sun 12–3.30 & 6–10.30, Underground: Southwark.* The large neon OXO sign marks the spot. Both the restaurant and brasserie on the 8th floor benefit from the 400m terrace for *al fresco* dining and superb views (*pictured overleaf*). The cooking here is excellent, with a fairly classic range using mainly British-sourced ingredients, with vegetarian and vegan alternatives, and an extensive, if somewhat intimidating, wine list with a selection of around 800 bottles. The brasserie is more laid back; you can slip in just for a drink at the bar, and a canapé.

£££ Skylon, *Royal Festival Hall, (**map p. 24, B2**), Tel: 020 7654 7800, restaurant open daily 12–2.30 & 5.30–10.45; grill open Sun–Wed 12–10.45, Thur–Sat 12–11.30, Underground: Waterloo.* Along with the rest of the refurbishments at the Royal Festival Hall, the restaurant has been revamped and named after the 88.4m steel and aluminium Skylon, the most iconic structure of the Festival of Britain in 1951. Subdued colours, surfaces of bronze, dark walnut and slate, and unusual chandeliers create a slick setting. In keeping with the seasonal modern British menu, using top-quality produce, created by head chef, Helene Puolakka. Signature dishes include Poached lobster with broad bean and cashew-nut salad, Confit of wild Scottish salmon, and *crepes suzette*. Good wine menu.

1 **££ Baltic**, *74 Blackfriars Road, Tel: 020 7928 1111, open Mon–Sat, 12–11, Sun 12–10.30, Underground: Southwark.* ■ This attractive restaurant specialising in eastern European-style food, is set in a converted 18th-century coachbuilders' workshop. The décor is uncluttered, its main feature being a splendid chandelier contrasting with a red brick wall. At the bar you can sample some of the 29 vodkas on offer and interesting bar snacks such as a blini selection. On the menu are hearty soups—Hungarian sour cherry or beetroot *Barszcz*, as well as dumplings, pigs' trotters, venison, and chicken *shashlik*.

2 **££ Magdalen**, *152 Tooley Street, Tel: 020 7403 1342, open Tues–Sat 12–2.15, Mon–Sat 6.30–10, Underground: London Bridge.* On two floors, painted in burgundy, the Magdalen arrived on the scene relatively recently and is fast making a name for itself as a serious restaurant. The young chefs here have combined their experience to create beautifully tuned dishes. The restaurant has a French feel but the food is predominantly British. The menu changes daily, there are dishes to share, and seasonal ingredients are Borough Market-sourced. Among the interesting choices are warm lentils, Pig's head brawn in a pot, Herefordshire snails, Lancashire hot-pot, and for afters Gingerbread ice-cream or Chestnut *millefeuilles*.

££ Roast, *The Floral Hall, Borough Market, (**map p. 25, B6**), Tel: 020 7940 1300, open Mon–Fri 7am–9.30am, 12–2.30pm & 5.30pm–10.30pm; Sat 8am–10.30am, 11.30–3.30 & 6pm–10.30pm; Sun midday–3.30, Underground: London Bridge.* ■ A massively popular

place, and with good reason, both for its unusual situation, suspended over Borough Market, and for the food. Open for breakfast, lunch and dinner, as well as 'Roast to go' breakfast butties and sandwiches, and afternoon tea Monday to Friday. It is built into the railway viaduct, looking down over the market on one side and Stoney Street on the other, while trains rumble overhead. As the name suggests, it specialises in succulent British spit roasts and grilled Laverstock Park organic rump steak. A great deal of research goes into sourcing the ingredients, from Orkney haggis to Isle of Wight garlic. The menu changes according to season and availability. The wine list includes English wines and good beers.

££ Tate Modern Restaurant, *Level 7, Tate Modern, (**map p. 25, B5**), Tel: 020 7887 8888, open Sun–Thur 10–6, Fri–Sat 10am–11pm, Underground: Southwark.* In a prime position on the 7th floor overlooking the Millennium Bridge and towards St Paul's Cathedral (*see p. 44*), the restaurant serves a wide selection of light snacks, three-course meals and afternoon tea. The cooking is based on seasonal, fresh products from Italy and Spain as well as the UK and has traditional touches such as Potted Cornish crab, Braised rabbit leg, and Brown sugar pavlova with clementines, or if you prefer, Cornish haddock and chips. There is an outside terrace for fine days.

Lunch with a view on the top floor of the Oxo Tower

3 **£ Masters Super Fish**, *191 Waterloo Road, Tel: 020 7928 6924, open Mon 5.30–10.30, Tues–Thur, Sat 12–3 & 4.30–10.30; Fri 12–3 & 4.30–11, Underground: Lambeth North, Waterloo.* If you want to indulge in a good example of one of Britain's most famous food combinations, fish'n'chips and mushy peas, this is the place to do it. Whether eat in or take away, tuck into crisp, battered haddock and fat chips, or settle for more sophisticated dressed crab or whitebait. Masters also happens to offer excellent puddings.

4 **£ The Table**, *83 Southwark Street, Tel: 020 7401 2760, open Mon–Thur 8–6, Fri 8–11, Sat 11–4; closed Sun, Underground: Southwark.* ■ You could almost walk by without noticing this understated, modern restaurant, on the ground floor of a company of architects. Straightforward and clean cut, like its name, it has a long counter, chunky wooden tables and an open kitchen. The service is friendly, as are the prices. Close to Tate Modern (see p. 27), it is a pleasing alternative to the bustle of Bankside. During the week there is a varied salad bar, and a take-away service. On Saturday brunch is served all day— the poached eggs in the Eggs Benedict are cooked to perfection. During the evening the atmosphere is more restaurant than café, with choices such as Slow roasted lamb, duck, steak with béarnaise sauce, and good traditional desserts.

shop

While you might be spoilt for choice for places to eat as well as shows and concerts to attend, the South Bank is not a shoppers' paradise. However, Borough Market and the boutiques at Oxo Tower Wharf more than make up for what the area might lack in other shopping departments. Shops are located on map pp. 24 & 25.

Borough Market, *Stoney Street, stalls open Thur 11–5, Fri 12–6, Sat 9–4, stalls closed Sun–Weds; Underground: London Bridge.* The market under the railway arches is one of the major attractions in this part of town, whether for shopping, eating or architectural viewing. The oldest of London's markets, it has occupied its present site since 1756. Borough draws visitors and shoppers not so much for its history but for the abundance and beauty of the gourmet products and the lively atmosphere. Around 70 densely packed stalls overflow with fish and meat, fruit and veg, bread and wine, as well as exotic cheeses, coffees and pastries and ready-to-eat food, from home and abroad. **Map p. 25, B6**

Oxo Tower Wharf, *Barge House Street, boutiques open Tues–Sun 11–6, Underground: Southwark.* An old power station, acquired in the 1920s by a meat extract company. As well as homes and restaurants (*see p. 37*), on the three lower levels are boutiques and galleries. Among them, on Level 1, is **Ian Bennett**, milliner, selling ready-to-wear or made-to-order hats and head-pieces, ranging from felt trilbies to the most elegant concoctions for a wedding or Ascot races; **Archipelago Textiles** selling wall hangings, bed covers and throws finely woven in subtle colours by Doreen Gittens, which can be made to order; **Eco-Annie** is full of eco-logically-friendly craft objects, knitwear, rugs and yarns; **Bagman and Robin** create a range of bags (which would go well with Ian Bennett's hats), both retro and whacky, for daytime or evening. On Level 2 are **Little & Collins'** beautiful handmade rugs and wall hangings; **Black + Blum**, an Anglo-Swiss design partnership, sells streamlined lighting and candlesticks and other innovatively designed objects. The **Llewellyn Alexander Gallery** sells original paintings, and **Vivienne Legg** specialises in hand-painted ceramics. **Map p. 24, B3**

a/s/e London

THE
CITY

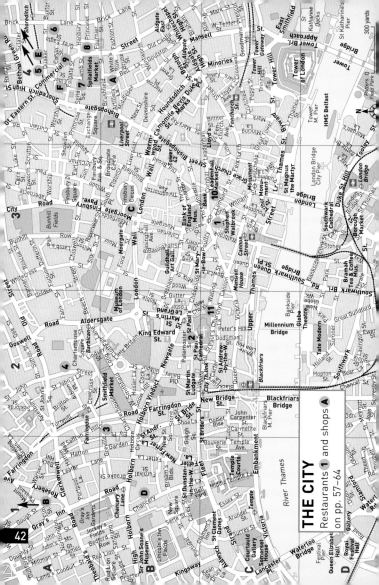

THE CITY

Restaurants **1** and shops **A**
on pp. 57–64

42

introduction

The City is where London began. The Romans settled here in AD 43 and constructed a bridge across the Thames, close to the present London Bridge, and the area quickly became the leading trading and financial centre it remains today. Originally demarcated by walls, sections are still visible at London Wall (*map opposite, B2–B3*). The City, or 'The Square Mile' as it is often referred to, maintains its own independence with an ancient constitution and livery companies, and a Lord Mayor (as opposed to the executive Mayor of London) elected each autumn since 1189.

Today, the densely packed City is going vertical. Following the Lloyd's of London insurance building in 1986, and the 'Gherkin' and Tower 42 more recently, some of the most innovative and highest structures in London are planned for the next few years.

During the week, the City throbs with activity but, unlike the West End or Westminster, it is deserted by its working population at weekends and the streets are relatively quiet. This is no disadvantage to visitors with such major historic monuments as St Paul's Cathedral and the Tower of London (officially just outside the City boundary) to get to grips with, as well as some less obvious monuments such as the handsome churches designed by Sir Christopher Wren, the Guildhall Art Gallery, the Museum of London, and the sedate Inns of Court at Temple.

Sunday is the main day to shop at some of the old markets, particularly Spitalfields, Brick Lane and Petticoat Lane, although weekdays are the best time to sample the City's penchant for champagne bars and excellent restaurants.

St Paul's Cathedral

Open: Daily 8.30–4, except during special services or events
Charges: Entry charge **Tel:** 020 7246 8357 **Web:** www.stpauls.co.uk
Underground: Bank, Mansion House, St Paul's **Map:** p. 42, B2–C2
Highlights: American Memorial Chapel; choir stalls; the dome and its galleries; Wellington monument; wrought iron by Jean Tijou

One of the most familiar silhouettes of London is the dome of St Paul's, Britain's major cathedral and the work of the eminent British architect Sir Christopher Wren. It stands grand and dignified at the top of Ludgate Hill, where it has been host to many significant events and celebrations, including Queen Victoria's Diamond Jubilee service in 1897, Winston Churchill's funeral in 1965, the marriage of Prince Charles and Lady Diana Spencer in 1981, and the present Queen's Golden Jubilee in 2002 and her 80th birthday in 2007. This cathedral is the fourth church on this site; the first was founded in 604.

An imposing flight of steps leads up to the two-tiered Corinthian portico of the cathedral, flanked by elaborate twin towers framing the dome. Three bells in the left tower include Great Paul, the biggest in Europe (it strikes at 1pm). The garden on the south-east offers the best view of the dome and lantern topped off by a gold ball and cross of 1821, stretching a total of 111.3m into the sky. The Golden Gallery at 85.4m is the highest level that visitors can climb–540 steps from the ground–whereas Wren was hauled up and down in a basket.

The interior

Nave and Chapels: The short wide nave, flanked by a three-bay run of rounded arches uses the Corinthian order and saucer domes, picked out elegantly in white, and leads the eye to the High Altar. Preceding the nave are All Soul's Chapel with a memorial to First World War Field-Marshal Lord Kitchener, and St Dunstan's Chapel, in memory of the Bishop of London and Archbishop of Canterbury (908–988). In the nave is the elaborate, multi-tiered **[A] Wellington monument** (1912) by Alfred Stevens to the military

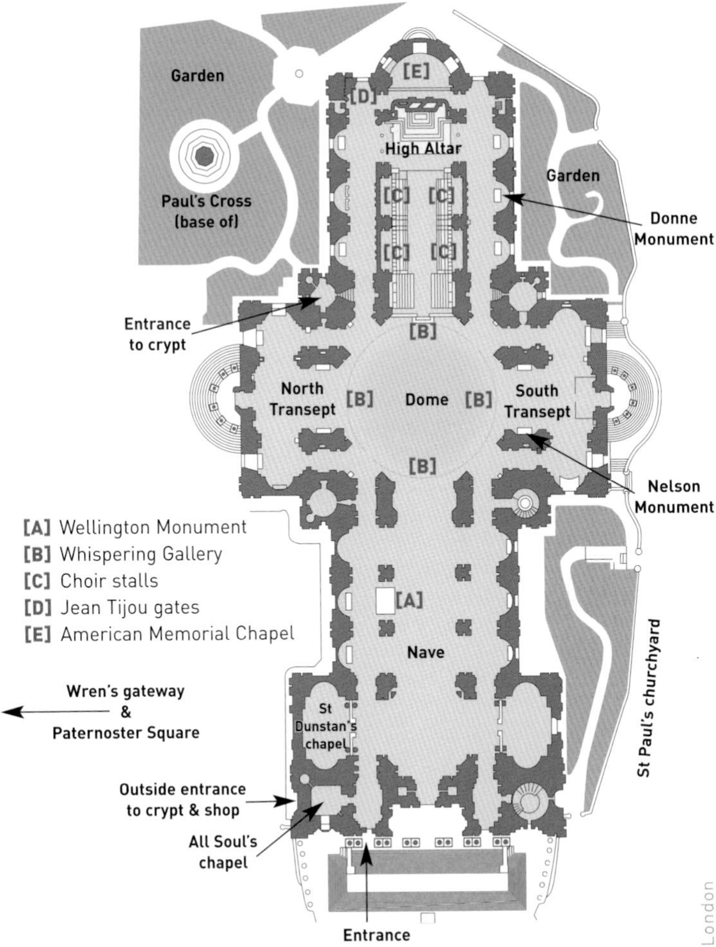

Garden

Paul's Cross
(base of)

[E]

[D]

High Altar

[C] [C]

[C] [C]

Garden

Donne
Monument

Entrance
to crypt

[B]

North
Transept [B] Dome [B] South
Transept

[B]

Nelson
Monument

[A] Wellington Monument
[B] Whispering Gallery
[C] Choir stalls
[D] Jean Tijou gates
[E] American Memorial Chapel

[A]

Wren's gateway
&
Paternoster Square

Nave

St
Dunstan's
chapel

St Paul's churchyard

Outside entrance
to crypt & shop

All Soul's
chapel

Entrance

leader and parliamentarian Duke of Wellington, which combines an equestrian statue of the Duke, a list of 48 battles, and a recumbent effigy (Wellington's remains are in the crypt below).

North transept and Dome: Pre-Raphaelite William Holman-Hunt's third version of *The Light of the World* (1900) hangs here, a detailed painting packed with religious symbolism. From here is a clear view of the superb **dome**, the second largest cathedral dome in Europe (after St Peter's in Rome) weighing about 65,000 tons. Its decoration includes mosaics of *Prophets* and *Saints* (1864–88) and the *Life of St Paul* painted in *grisaille trompe l'oeil* in 1715 by James Thornhill, as well as excessive High Victorian mosaics and gilding (1890), added after Queen Victoria deemed the interior of the church 'dingy [and] undevotional'. Around the drum supporting the dome runs the [B] **Whispering Gallery**, 259 steps up, with remarkable acoustics which allow a whisper against the wall on one side to be heard clearly on the opposite side. On the exterior of the dome, a further 119 steps higher, is the **Stone Gallery** (53.4m), and 152 steps more, past the brick cone,

is the **Golden Gallery**, for a bird's eye view of London.

Choir and Choir Aisles: The [C] **choir stalls** (*guided visits only*), like the organ case (1659), were carved in a variety of woods by the most sought-after 18th-century woodcarver, Grinling Gibbons, with cherubs, flowers and fruits of extraordinary beauty and naturalness. The high altar (1958) and canopy were remade after the Victorian version was damaged by bombs (St Paul's famously survived the Blitz relatively unscathed). In the north choir aisle are superb [D] **wrought iron** gates by French Protestant craftsman, Jean Tijou, and the strikingly pure *Mother and Child* (1984) carved in stone by Henry Moore. The roll of honour in the [E] **American Memorial Chapel** (1958) with the names of 28,000 American Service personnel who died during World War II, was presented by President Eisenhower. The stained glass windows (1960) represent *Service*, *Sacrifice* and *Resurrection*, and a rocket carved in the panelling pays tribute to America's space research. Wren's original high altar stands in the Lady Chapel, and in the south choir aisle is

Sir Christopher Wren (1632–1723)

Academic, master architect, member of Parliament, President of the Royal Society, and one of London's most influential figures. 'A miracle of youth' is how the diarist and scholar John Evelyn saw Sir Christopher Wren. Certainly, by the time Wren had reached middle age, he had achieved more than others had accomplished in their lifetimes; he was just 31 years old and already a respected architect when he came to survey the neglected St Paul's cathedral and, over a series of years, submitted to Charles II six different plans for its renovation, including a revised design for the entire city of London (which was rejected due to concerns over the timespan of the project).

The son of a learned clergyman who held the position of Dean of Windsor, Wren spent some of his childhood as a playmate of the Prince of Wales (later Charles II); a relationship which would prove significant for Wren in his architectural career. Wren's first career, however, was an academic one, as Professor of astronomy and maths at Oxford University. It wasn't until 1663 that he received his first architectural commission, from his uncle, the Bishop of Ely, to design a new chapel for Pembroke College, Cambridge.

The Great Fire of London in 1666 undoubtedly made Wren the public figure he is today. He was appointed to the official rebuilding commission by Charles II, who accepted his plans for St Paul's as well as those for 51 of the 87 churches (*see p. 56*) destroyed during the fire. St Paul's and the City churches are unique works by one man. While working on these major projects, he also constructed London's Monument to the Great Fire (*see p. 54*), carried out work on the White Tower at the Tower of London (*see p. 49*), the veterans hospitals at Greenwich and Chelsea (*see p. 132*), and supervised alterations and repairs to the House of Commons, Westminster Abbey (*see p. 105*), St James's Palace and Whitehall Palace.

Fittingly, when Wren died at the age of 90, he was the first person to be buried in St Paul's Cathedral.

London

a/s/e

the monument (1631) by Nicholas Stone to the poet John Donne, the only monument to survive the Great Fire of London in 1666. It shows Donne, the most famous Dean of St Paul's (1631–32), dressed in a shroud.

South transept: Remembered here are prominent figures of British history: Dr Johnson, J.M.W. Turner, and Admiral Nelson whose magnificent monument (1805) is by the renowned British sculptor, John Flaxman.

Crypt: Part of the medieval cathedral, the vast crypt underpins the full length of the present building and is the repository of many famous souls. A plain marble slab marks the grave of Sir Christopher Wren, with the inscription that translates 'If you seek his monument, look around you'. In the centre of the crypt lie Admiral Nelson, in a tomb designed in the 16th century for Cardinal Wolsey, and the Duke of Wellington. Others remembered here include Florence Nightingale.

Temple Bar

Wren's gateway (1672), used to mark the formal entrance to the City, at the junction of Fleet Street and the Strand (*map p. 42, C1*), and is the only surviv-ing example of a City gate in London. Too narrow for the increasing traffic, it was dismantled in the late 1800s and bought by a wealthy family to adorn their country estate in Hertfordshire. The gateway has now been magnificent-ly restored, returned to the City and erected in Paternoster Square oppo-site St Paul's cathedral, in honour of Wren.

Tower of London

Open: Mon–Fri 9–5, Sun & holidays 10–5 **Charges:** Entry charge
Tel: 0844 482 7777 (bookings only) **Web:** www.hrp.org.uk
Underground: Tower Hill **Map:** p. 42, C4–D4
Highlights: Crown Jewels; guided tours by Yeoman Warders;
reconstructed Medieval Palace; White Tower

The Tower of London, on the banks of the river Thames, is a perfect
English medieval fortress. Since Britain's early history it has served as
palace, prison and place of execution at the very heart of the defence
of the Royal Crown. Today, it is the repository of the priceless Crown
Jewels, the ravens who have patrolled the Tower for over 900 years,
and home to the historic Yeoman Warders, or 'Beefeaters', who have
protected the Royal Family since 1509. The Tower also houses a
superb collection of royal armouries.

The Tower of London takes its name from the White Tower, the central and oldest part of the stronghold, commissioned by William the
Conqueror after the Battle of Hastings in 1066. Successive monarchs
expanded and reconstructed the Tower area by strengthening defenses
and building more towers. It has been the location for numerous royal
murders, most famously, the young princes, Edward V and his brother
Richard, in 1483. Other royals fell victim to the executioner's block on
Tower Green, particularly under the reign of Henry VIII and his
daughter 'Bloody' Mary. By the 17th century the Tower became more
arsenal than prison, and the Victorians did their best to take the
Tower back to its medieval palace past and turned it into the tourist
attraction it is today.

The Tower resembles a small village, and to do justice to your visit
it is worth putting aside a whole day; pre-booking is recommended.
Be prepared for long queues to view the Crown Jewels. The ceremonial
Opening of the Tower takes place at 9am, in full view of waiting visitors. (The Ceremony of the Keys in the evening is for limited numbers;
apply in writing). There are places to eat and shop both inside and
outside the walls.

a/s/e London

Tower of London

Lanthorn Tower

Reconstructed Medieval Palace

[A] Byward Tower
[B] Traitors' Gate
[C] White Tower
     (Royal Armouries)
[D] Crown Jewels
     (Waterloo Barracks)
[E] Tower Green
[F] Beauchamp Tower
[G] Bloody Tower

Queen's House

Yeoman Warder guided tours start here

Entrance

Bell Tower

Street

Mint

Chapel of St Peter ad Vincula

Lane

Water

N

[A] Byward Tower: With its impressive original portcullis, this is a fitting main entrance to the Tower of London. Byward Tower is normally closed to the public but it's well worth asking one of the Yeoman Warders to see inside for the 15th-century painted chimneybreast and walls. In 1747 it was the prison of Lord Lovat, the last person to be beheaded in England. The Bell Tower opposite is where the young Princess Elizabeth (later Queen Elizabeth I) was confined for several weeks for her alleged part in the conspiracy to overthrow her half-sister, Mary I. Mint Street is named for the Royal Mint which was established at the Tower in the 13th century; its most famous Master of the Mint was Isaac Newton who lived here in 1699. It is now home to the **Yeoman Warders**, who give excellent tours of the Tower. Queen's House, the windows of which overlook Water Lane, is where Guy Fawkes was interrogated and tortured in 1605 for his part in the attempted destruction of Parliament.

[B] Traitors' Gate: Illustrious prisoners such as Henry VIII's second wife, Anne Boleyn, passed through Traitors' Gate and up to St Thomas's Tower, which is now the entrance to the **reconstructed Medieval Palace**. Henry III made St Thomas's Tower a rich royal residence for the first time. To evoke the period the display includes replicas of period furnishings and a rotating exhibition of medieval objects in the Lanthorn Tower.

[C] White Tower: The oldest building in London was commissioned by William the Conqueror after the Battle of Hastings in 1066 to defend his newly-conquered territory, and to inspire fear in both Londoners and potential foreign invaders. A massively strong 27m-high Norman structure, the base of the walls are 4.5m thick. It acquired its name in the 13th century when Henry III had it whitewashed. Since its construction, it has been much restored, including the alteration of its windows by Sir Christopher Wren. The beautiful Norman chapel inside, dedicated to St John the Evangelist, is the oldest church in London (1087), and was host to Lady Jane Grey during her nine-day reign, and Mary I's betrothal by proxy to Philip of Spain. The magnificent collection of Royal armouries in the other rooms of the Tower

a/s/e London

include the armour of the Tudor and Stuart kings and princes, notably an enormous suit engraved by Hans Holbein the Younger for Henry VIII.

[D] Crown Jewels: This spectacular display is housed in the strongroom of the 19th-century Waterloo Barracks. Last used at Queen Elizabeth II's coronation in 1953, the regalia date mainly from 1660 onwards—Cromwell had the gold and silver melted down during the Commonwealth and only three swords and the silver gilt Coronation Spoon survived. The Orb and Sceptre have been used at every coronation since that of Charles II (1660). Among the awe-inspiring array of crowns is St Edward's Crown (1661), which is employed for the crowning of each sovereign, The oldest items, the Ampulla and Spoon, are used for the anointing of the sovereign by the Archbishop. The Sceptre contains the largest top-quality cut diamond in the world, *Cullinan 1*. The *Koh-i-Noor* was given to Queen Victoria in 1849 by the Maharajah of Lahore, and placed in the platinum crown worn by the late Queen Mother at George VI's coronation. The lightest is Queen Victoria's Diamond Crown, designed to be worn on her widow's cap. The Imperial State Crown, worn at the State opening of Parliament, contains a sapphire from Edward the Confessor's ring.

[E] Tower Green: The former site of politically sensitive beheadings of high-ranking individuals. Catherine Howard, fifth wife of Henry VIII, was accused of adultery and beheaded in 1542 along with her lady-in-waiting, Jane, Viscountess Rochford. Those executed here were buried in the nearby Chapel Royal of St Peter ad Vincula.

[F] Beauchamp Tower: The walls of the upper chamber inside this tower are covered with graffiti etched by prisoners throughout the Tower's history, including Lady Jane Grey.

[G] Bloody Tower: This is traditionally the site of the murder of the Princes in the Tower: Edward IV's young sons, Edward V and Richard, Duke of York. The Bloody Tower was reserved for noble prisoners, such as Sir Walter Raleigh. He was imprisoned here three times. On his second visit, Raleigh was confined for 13 years in relative comfort. Accompanied by his wife and children, he grew tobacco and wrote *The History of the World* (1614).

Tower Bridge

Open: Daily April–Sept 10–6.30, Oct–March 9.30–6 **Charges:** Entry charge **Tel:** 020 7403 3761 **Web:** www.towerbridge.org.uk
Underground: London Bridge, Tower Hill **Map:** p. 42, D4.
Highlight: View from high walkway

This icon of London, designed by engineer John Wolfe Barry and architect Horace Jones, opened in 1894 and was the first crossing downstream of London Bridge. The mock-Gothic towers disguise suspension cables and lifts, and a sophisticated mechanism for raising the *bascules*—arms—of the lower bridge. The bridge now only opens by arrangement and is an impressive sight. The visit begins in the north tower, where visitors ascend to the high walkway to enjoy the river views, taking in the Tower of London (*see p. 49*), St Paul's Cathedral (*see p. 44*) and the London Eye (*see p. 33*), as well as sights further afield such as London's Docklands and Greenwich. The tour continues in the basement of the south tower amid the cast-iron boilers and flywheels of the mechanical lifting gear, a triumph of Victorian engineering but sadly consigned to the museum when electricity was introduced in 1976.

a/s/e London

Guildhall Art Gallery (*open Mon–Sat 10–5, Sun 12–4, entry charge, Tel: 020 7332 3700, Web: www.guildhall-art-gallery.org.uk, Underground: Bank, Moorgate*). The Corporation of London's collection is little-known but is a fascinating insight into the city through its art. Among cherished works are full-length portraits of two *Fire Judges* who assessed property claims after the Great Fire of London in 1666, by John Michael Wright (1670). Views of London include William Lionel Wyllie's *The Opening of Tower Bridge* (1894–95). Among several popular Pre-Raphaelite works is *The Woodman's Daughter* (1851) by John Everett Millais, and Dante Rossetti's *La Ghirlandata* (1871–74). Edwin Landseer's *The First Leap* (1829) and James Tissot's *The Last Evening* (1873) are also shown here. Traces of Roman London's amphitheatre (c. AD 70–4th century), surprisingly unearthed in 1987, can be viewed beneath the gallery. **Map p. 42, B3**

Lloyd's of London (*private building, no entry, Underground: Aldgate, Monument*). Considered a pioneering example of British high-tech architecture, the Lloyd's building (1978–86) at One Lime Street was designed by Richard Rogers (architect of the Pompidou Centre in Paris, and Heathrow airport's Terminal 5) to house Lloyd's of London, the world's leading marine insurance market. Essential services are on the exterior for ease of access and to provide maximum space inside, where a cathedral-like 12-floor glass atrium, naturally lit, is crossed by escalators. At its core, overlooked by galleries, is the four-storey Underwriting Room (the 'Room') where, until 1989, the Lutine Bell, salvaged from a French Ship in 1793, signalled good news with one strike and bad with two. The glassed-in upper floors are accessed externally by the first glass lifts in Britain. The 11th floor Committee Room contains the original dining room (1763), transferred from the company's previous building. **Map p. 42, C4**

Monument (*closed for refurbishment until December 2008, normally open daily 9.30–5.30, entry charge, Underground: Cannon Street, Monument*). The Monument was erected 1671–76 by Sir Christopher Wren to mark the Great Fire of London in 1666. A fluted Doric column of Portland stone, its height of 61.6m makes it the tallest stand-alone column in the world. The height signifies the distance to Pudding Lane, where the fire began in a bake house on 2nd September. Inside are 311 steps to the square balcony, above which is a cupola supporting a flaming urn of copper. On the west side of the plinth is a relief of the ruined City. The fire, not an uncommon event in 17th-century London, caused huge devastation due to a brisk southeast wind and a damaged main water pump under London Bridge. In 72 hours the Guildhall, St Paul's Cathedral, 13,000 houses and shops, 44 livery halls and 87 churches were destroyed. Remarkably, only nine lives were recorded lost. Wren was a member of the Commission for the remarkably swift reconstruction programme. **Map p. 42, C3**

Museum of London (*open Mon–Sat 10–5.50, Sun 12–5.50, lower galleries closed for redevelopment until 2009, free entry, Tel: 0870 444 3581, Web: www.museumoflondon.org.uk, Underground: Barbican, Moorgate, St Paul's*). A wide-ranging group of objects, from bus tickets to a bank, lead you through the remarkable history of London from its prehistoric beginnings, c. 500,000 years ago, to the present. Among the museum's collection of 1 million items are bronze weapons dredged from the river Thames, a King Alfred silver penny (c. 886), medieval pilgrim badges and pointy shoes, the Cheapside Hoard of jewellery hidden in the mid-seven-

Middle Temple Lodge, part of the medieval Inns of Court complex at Temple

a/s/e London

teenth century and not discovered until 1912, and Oliver Cromwell's Bible. The museum is located very close to sections of the Roman wall which once marked the limits of the city. **Map p. 42, B2**

Temple (*courts open to the public, gardens occasionally open 12.30–3, buildings closed, Underground: Temple*). Enter the Inner Temple Court via Falcon Street, or Inner Temple Lane through the 16th-century entrance to discover the reserve of lawyers in the City: a medieval maze of gas-lit passages and courtyards. Here, in the 12th century, the Knights Templar built their New Temple church and monastery. Discredited for their power and wealth in the 14th century, the Templar property was leased to lawyers as Inns of Court, hostels for barristers and students. The Round Church of the Templars (*occasionally open to the public; Tel: 020 7353 3470*), in transitional Norman-Gothic style, dates back to c. 1185. The fine rectangular chancel, added 1220–40, was embellished by Sir Christopher Wren. It contains important (restored) Crusader monuments. King's Bench Walk has an impressive collection of 17th-century houses. Middle Temple Hall (1560) (*to view, ask at the porter's lodge*), has a superb oak double-hammer-beam roof and huge bench table, and was the setting for the first performance of Shakespeare's *Twelfth Night* in 1602. **Map p. 42, C1**

Wren Churches (*open Mon–Fri 10.30 or 11 until 4.30 or 6.30*). Eighty six of 107 City churches were destroyed by the Great Fire of London in 1666, and Sir Christopher Wren was subsequently involved with rebuilding 51 of them over 46 years. Of the most interesting, **St Stephen Walbrook** (*map p. 42, C3*) has a centrally-planned layout enclosed in a rectangle, and a superb dome, supported by Corinthian columns. **St Mary-le-Bow** (*map p.42, C3*), or Bow church, has a steeple of masterly elegance (1679) topped by a gold dragon weathervane. True Londoners claim to be only those born within the sound of Bow Bells. **St Martin Ludgate** (*map p. 42, B2*) has a handsome interior, and **St Andrew-by-the-Wardrobe** (*map p. 42, C2*)—wardrobe being the Crown clothing store under Edward III—was Wren's last city church. **St Bride's** (*map p. 42, C2*), has the tallest Wren steeple, built in tiers like a wedding cake, and **St Dunstan in the West** (*map p. 42, D1*), has a tower medieval in inspiration. **St Magnus the Martyr** (*map p. 42, C3*), has a tower reminiscent of a Belgian Jesuit church, and a rich collection of 17th-century woodwork inside. Just outside the eastern City boundary is the important **St Clement Danes** (*map p. 42, C1*) which was not a rebuild (the Great Fire of London did not reach this far). It is the only Wren church (except St Paul's Cathedral; *see p. 44*) to have a double apse.

eat

Eating in the city is strictly a weekday affair, with restaurants and pubs full at lunchtime with city workers, and champagne and luxury gourmet provided at night. The central markets supply ingredients to many City restaurants such as St John near Smithfield meat market. Perhaps the understated star of this area is Brick Lane for its concentration of curry houses. For price categories, see p. 11; all restaurants are located on map p. 42.

ST PAULS

1 ££ 1 Lombard Street - the Brasserie, *1 Lombard Street, Tel: 020 7939 6611, open Mon–Fri 7.30am–10pm, Underground: Bank.* If ever there was a bankers' address, this is it, and if 'power lunches' were still fashionable, they would be here. The circular bar and busy brasserie are in a Neoclassical banking hall, covered by a glass dome. This is a smart place to eat, with efficient service and satisfying food, both simple and elaborate, from Bangers and mash to Coq au vin. There is a separate dining area that is quieter but a little more expensive.

2 ££ Paternoster Chop House, *Warwick Court, Paternoster Square, Tel: 020 7029 9400, open Mon–Fri 12–3 & 5.30–10.30, Underground: St Paul's.* Exceedingly City (notably the prices), and British (the ingredients), the Chop House holds the trump card when it comes to its situation, across from St Paul's

cathedral. The cooking is spot on and the menu changes with the seasons. The Potted crab, Mendip lamb and Newlyn cod are all excellent when available, and there are also the good old favourites such as Bubble and squeak, Cottage pie, and, for afters, Bakewell tart and clotted cream. What more could you ask for?

£ The Place Below, *St Mary-le-Bow church (**map p. 42, C3**), Tel: 020 7329 0789, open Mon–Fri 7.30–3, lunch from 11.30, Underground: Bank, St Paul's.* If a devotee of Wren and a vegetarian, where better to have lunch than in the crypt of one of Wren's City churches (see p. 56 opposite). Here, you'll eat in the true heart of London—within the sound of the Bow Bells. The choice is not exhaustive but the canteen-style food is fresh, changes daily and is good value for money. The crunchy salads are excellent and the soup is filling.

a/s/e London

SMITHFIELD

③ ££ Bleeding Heart, *Bleeding Heart Yard, off Greville Street, Tel: 020 7242 2056, open Mon–Fri 12–2.30 & 6–10.30, Underground: Chancery Lane, Farringdon.* Discreetly hidden in a courtyard, the décor is sophisticated wood and leather, and dress should not be too casual. Lunchtime clientele consists mainly of well-heeled City types, but in the evening the ambiance is more romantic. The seasonal menu, described as French, has a few British touches, including savouries: suckling pig and smoked eels. It is all extremely good and the service impeccable.

④ ££ St John Restaurant, *26 St John Street, Tel: 020 7251 0848, open Mon–Fri 12–3 & 6–11; Sat 6–11, Underground: Farringdon.* St John opened in 1994 in a Georgian building used until 1967 as a smoke house. Be prepared for the almost severe setting. Close to Smithfield meat market, the menu has a decidedly carnivorous theme, and specialises in unfashionable cuts of meat and offal, cooked imaginatively and to perfection. These might include (according to season) roast bone marrow, crispy pig's skin, ox tongue and roast mutton, excellent terrines and charcuterie.

SPITALFIELDS AND BRICK LANE

£££ Rhodes Twenty Four, *Tower 42, 25 Old Broad Street, (map p. 42, B3), Tel: 020 7877 7703, open Mon–Fri 12–2.30 & 6–9, Underground: Liverpool Street.* The English-style cooking on the 24th floor, by chef Adam Gray, is high standard and well balanced. The plain, geometric setting is designed not to be invasive or get in the way of the stunning views. Dishes on the menu might include Seared cep mushroom tartlet, Jerusalem artichoke and walnut salad, Saddle of rabbit with braised pearl barley rabbit risotto, and even Bread and butter pudding.

⑤ ££ Loungelover, *1 Whitby Street, Tel: 020 7012 1234, open Sun–Thur 6pm–midnight, Fri 5.30pm–1am, Sat 6pm–1am, Underground: Shoreditch.* ■ An Outrageously kitsch cocktail lounge (*pictured opposite*), in a former meat-packing factory, with themed spaces (such as luscious red or classic Baroque), and highly innovative cocktails. It is one of three bars under the Trois Garcons umbrella (1 Club Row, Brick Lane), and has bar food to keep you going.

⑥ £ Bengal Village, *75 Brick Lane, Tel: 020 7366 4868, open daily 12–12, Underground: Aldgate East, Liverpool Street.* Where else to eat curry than Brick Lane? Bengal Village serves not only ordinary curries, but also more refined authentic Bangladeshi varieties. The Naga lamb marinated with green chillies, and the Laboni

Kitsch design at cocktail bar Loungelover, in a former meat-packing factory

Sabzi vegetables with almonds and coconut are worth sampling.

7 £ Canteen, *2 Crispin Place, Tel: 0845 686 1122, open Mon–Fri 8am–11pm, Sat & Sun 9am–11pm, Underground: Liverpool Street.* ■ Directly-sourced, additive-free ingredients go into British classics such as Lamb with mint sauce, Chicken and mushroom pie (or veggie pie), and Seabass with caper and parsley sauce and, as a starter, fashionable beetroot, celeriac and horseradish in a generous portion. Puddings are even better than Mum used to make (orange jelly, treacle tart, rice pudding). Noisy and more cheerful than a works canteen.

8 £ Golden Heart, *110 Commercial Street, Tel: 020 7247 2158, open Mon–Sat 11–11, Sun 11am–10.30pm, Underground: Aldgate East.* A hearty, noisy, old-fashioned pub between Brick Lane and Spitalfields with an open fire.

9 £ Hawksmoor, *157 Commercial Street, Tel: 020 7247 7392, open Mon–Thur 12–12, Fri 12pm–1am, Sat 6pm–1am, Underground: Liverpool Street.* Nicholas Hawksmoor, pupil of Wren, was responsible for Christ Church Spitalfields. Hawksmoor, the restaurant, beckons for a convivial drink, or for an excellent steak, but preferably both. An American-style haunt, it has great cocktails and American music, but these are just side orders to what is really important here: the steak. The beef from Yorkshire is superb.

Champagne in the City

Well-heeled imbibers in the City revel in champagne and cocktails at flash, modern venues, with smart dress codes.

10 Abacus (*24 Cornhill, Tel: 0871 223 1028, open Mon–Wed 12–12, Thur–Fri 12pm–2am, Underground: Bank*), is one such venue with three bars and two floors, DJ and dancing, cocktails and food. **11 Dion Champagne** (*Paternoster House, 65 St Paul's Churchyard, Tel: 0871 971 4020, open Mon–Tues 10am–11pm, Wed–Fri 10am–1am, Underground: St Paul's*). The Dion group's most recent happening bar is next to St Paul's cathedral. Here you can indulge in a glass of Bollinger Grande Année 1996 or Krug, while nibbling on a sandwich and enjoying good music. **Vertigo 42** (*Tower 42, 25 Old Broad Street, Tel: 020 7877 7842, open Mon–Fri, 12–3 & 5–11, Underground: Bank, Liverpool Street; map p. 42, B3*). The uncomplicated décor concentrates the mind on the 360° views (*pictured below*) and a selective menu is designed to match the vintages.

And while on the subject, the longest (90m) champagne bar in the capital is on the upper floor of London's most glamorous station, St Pancras International (*off map p. 67, A7*).

shop

The City of London may not be the first place that springs to mind for a good day's retail therapy, but the old, established markets in this part of London provide fascinating opportunities to browse and buy, from bric-a-brac at Brick Lane to fine food at Leadenhall. Outside of the markets, Hatton Garden (*map p. 42, A1–B1*) is the place to buy gold and diamond jewellery, whereas the shops in the City provide all you need in executive ware to relieve you of your cash. All shops are located on map p. 42.

MARKETS

Brick Lane, *open Sun 8–2, Underground: Aldgate East, Aldgate.* Typical of East End London, Brick Lane is a real mix of cultures, epitomised by the mosque on the corner of Fournier Street: built as a Huguenot church in 1740, taken over by the Methodists in 1809, transformed into a synagogue in 1897, until in 1976 it assumed its present role. Brick Lane was the setting for Monica Ali's book of the same name about British Asians, and the ethnic mix is reflected in the choice of restaurants and market wares. The flea market is pretty chaotic, and brings out the bargain hunters. With diligent searching, you might pick up a gem among the clothes, furniture or general junk. **Map p. 42, A4–B4**

Leadenhall, *1 Leadenhall Place, open Mon–Fri 7–4, Underground: Bank, Monument.* Leadenhall

acquired its name in the 14th century from a mansion with a lead roof, but mansion and market were burned down in 1666. The replacement market had three large yards: the beef market, which sold leather, wool and raw hide; the veal, mutton and lamb market, also fish, poultry and cheese; and the herb market, for fruit and vegetables. The present Victorian building (1881) of wrought-iron and glass was designed by Horace Jones (also Billingsgate and Smithfield markets), and is still a mainly produce market. On sale is some of the finest food in London, including meat, poultry, game and fish. Close to Lloyd's of London (*see p. 54*) and the Bank of England, at midday City workers pour in. Especially popular is The Lamb Tavern (*Tel: 020 7626 2454*), established in 1780, with upstairs dining. **Map p. 42, C3**

a/s/e London

Petticoat Lane, *between Middlesex & Goulston Streets* (*map p. 42, B2*) *open Sun 9–2; a smaller market, Mon–Fri, is held on Wentworth Street, Underground: Aldgate, Aldgate East.* Petticoat Lane was already an old-clothes market in the early 17th century, when Huguenot silk weavers were selling their wares. The Great Plague of 1665 drove out the upper classes from this fashionable area and Jewish traders moved in later, so that by the 1750s it was a well-established trading centre. Although the street was renamed in 1846, the more appropriate Petticoat Lane is still used for the inexpensive clothes market, for which it's so well known. All types of fashions are sold, especially leather goods. With around 1,000 or so stalls on a Sunday morning, stamina is required for searching and haggling for bargains amongst the many shoppers.

Smithfield, *Charterhouse Street, open Mon–Fri 4am–midday, Underground: Barbican, Farringdon.* London's oldest market, which has traded in meat for some 800 years stands on a site which has hosted a cattle market since the 10th century. Housed in a listed Victorian building, the whole site has undergone a £70-million refit to make it the most advanced, state-of-the-art meat market in Europe, including sealed delivery bays and robotic sorting mechanisms. However, visitors can still wander the central aisles of the market and see the huge range of produce on offer. Smithfield market also sells cheeses and delicatessen goods, not only to butchers, but to restaurateurs and caterers. **Map p. 42, B2**

Spitalfields, *Brushfield Street, stalls open 10–4, shops 11–7 (may vary): Mon, Tues & Sat shops, no stalls; Wed traders market, 1st & 3rd of month records & books; Thur antiques & vintage objects; Fri: fashion and art; Sun 9–5, all shops and stalls, Underground: Aldgate East, Liverpool Street.* Trading goes back to 13th century at this most important of wholesale fruit and vegetable markets, to the extent that in 1991 the produce section moved to another more spacious location in London. The building revamped its image and the whole area has experienced something of a revival, attracting modern designers, artists and craftsmen. The old covered market is at its liveliest on Sunday with around 200 stalls and shops selling everything from way-out fashions to organic food. Friday Fun Fashion Market is the opportunity for up-and-coming young designers to show off, and hopefully sell, their creations. Weekdays are less busy, except at lunchtime. Christ Church Spitalfields, a fine church by Nicholas Hawksmoor, is the focus of an annual music festival. **Map p. 42, A4**

Bric-a-brac on sale at Brick Lane market, in London's East End

a/s/e London

SHOPS IN THE CITY

Ⓐ A Gold, *42 Brushfield Street, Tel: 020 7247 2487, open Mon–Fri 11–8, Sun 11–6, closed Sat, Underground: Liverpool Street.* A tiny deli fully packed with good things to eat, it famously stocks entirely the sort of goods Brits grow up with: chutney, Dorset Knobs, Banbury Cakes and Dundee Cake as well as additive-free bacon, and Bramley Apple Juice, Dandelion and Burdock, and Elderberry Port.

Ⓑ EC One, *41 Exmouth Market, Tel: 020 7713 6185, open Mon–Wed & Fri 9–6, Thur 10–7, Sat 10.30–6, Underground: Farringdon.* This is a smart, modern goldsmith not far from the Hatton Garden diamond and jewellery area of London. EC One is their original boutique where you can watch the designers at work and receive personalised service. Beautiful objects include fashion and precious items, as well as engagement rings and wedding bands. They also showcase the work of around 20 other designers.

Ⓒ Flittner, *82 Moorgate, Tel: 020 7606 4750, open Mon–Wed, Fri 8–6, Thur 8–6.30, Underground: Liverpool Street, Moorgate.* Established in 1904, the city gentlemen's barber's shop remains delightfully old-fashioned with engraved glass cabinets and marble basins. Gentlemen may still luxuriate in a hot towel shave, if requested, or a straight-forward shampoo and cut, or beard trim, as well as purchase toiletries.

Ⓓ London Silver Vaults, *53–64 Chancery Lane, Tel: 020 7242 3844, open Mon–Fri 9–5.30, Sat 9–1, Underground: Chancery Lane.* A variety of shops and an enormous stock of silver and silver plate, antique and modern; this is an Aladdin's cave of silverware for large or small purchases. The reputation of the vaults and the excellent service provided has spread throughout the world. The vaults originally opened in 1876 to provide strongboxes for the storage of valuables. Gradually the focus shifted to dealers who sought safe premises, and this role escalated during the Second World War. The Silver Vaults have remained unchanged since 1953.

Ⓔ Luna & Curious, *198 Brick Lane, Tel: 07977 440212, open daily 12–7, Underground: Aldgate East, Liverpool Street.* This is an exotic address selling the output of a collective of eight designers who come up with some unusual and quirky pieces, all unique. It includes ceramics, jewellery, vintage clothing, textiles, ornaments and men's accessories.

Ⓕ Timothy Everest, *32 Elder Street, Tel: 020 7377 3770, open Mon–Fri 9–6, alternate Sat 9–4, Underground: Liverpool Street.* A successful young London tailor whose designs are stylish and relaxed, using a mix of colours and interesting combinations of fabric. He even customises denim.

BLOOMSBURY & THE WEST END

BLOOMSBURY & THE WEST END

Restaurants **1** and shops **A**
on pp. 88–94

66

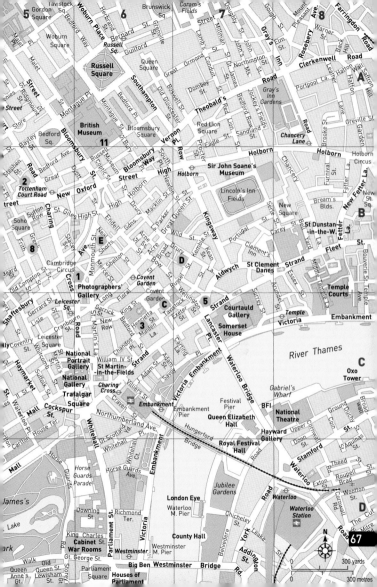

introduction

Bloomsbury, eminently intellectual and creative, was the base for both the Bloomsbury Group of writers, critics and artists who held their salons in Gordon Square (*map p. 67, A5*), and the Pre-Raphaelite Brotherhood, whose founder, John Everett Millais, had his family home close by, on Gower Street. Today, the elegant straight streets and squares are home to University College London and the British Museum.

The West End has always evoked wealth, commerce, luxury and leisure and for some 200 years has been associated with shopping and entertainment, notably opera and theatre. To the west of the City, it became the residential area of the moneyed classes after the Great Fire of London in 1666, when the beautiful squares and handsome terraces were developed. One of the most ancient thoroughfares, now known as Oxford Street (*map p. 66, B1–67, B6*), was in fact developed in the late-18th century by the Earl of Oxford, Edward Harley, and never did lead to Oxford. Apart from shopping, the West End has some of the most important museums and galleries in London including the National Gallery, the National Portrait Gallery, the Courtauld Gallery at Somerset House, and the Wallace Collection.

This area's restaurants are legion. Soho (reputedly named after the cry of the medieval huntsmen when this was farmland) is a dense and enclosed area and has increasingly become one of the best places to eat and drink in town. Chinatown is a small section of Soho, whose Chinese connections go back to the early 20th century and developed after the Second World War. Centred on Gerrard Street (*map p. 67, C5*), it is decorated with colourful archways and packed with Chinese restaurants.

British Museum

Open: Mon–Wed 10–5.30, Thur, Fri & Sat, 9–11, Sun 10–6; closed
1 Jan, Good Friday, 24–26 Dec **Charges:** Free entry, except special
exhibitions **Tel:** 020 7323 9299 **Web:** www.britishmuseum.org
Underground: Goodge Street, Russell Square **Map:** 67, A6
Highlights: Assyrian sculpture (Ancient Near East); Elgin Marbles
(Greece); Hoa Hakananai'a statue (Oceania); Mildenhall Treasure
(European Prehistory); Rosetta Stone (Egypt); Townley Marbles
(Roman)

The British Museum is a veritable treasure trove of rare and beautiful art
and antiquities which span two million years of world history and a wide
range of cultures. The collection began in 1753 with the manuscripts,
library and specimens of Hans Sloane, president of the Royal Society,
physician and botanist. With important acquisitions in the late 18th and
early 19th centuries, such as the Rosetta Stone and the Elgin Marbles, the
museum grew to become the leading secular public museum in the world.

Robert Smirke's Greek Revival building of 1852 has an impressive
Ionic colonnaded façade overlooking a large courtyard. The interior
quadrangle, or Great Court, formerly home to the British Library
(transferred to St Pancras in 2000; *see p. 86*), was transformed by
Norman Foster's glass roof, and has become the hub of the museum
with shops, cafes, restaurant and special exhibition galleries.

It is difficult to see everything in the British Museum in one day.
Following is a selection of the highlights in the collection:

Greek and Roman Antiquities
(*rooms 11–23, 67–73, 77–85*):
One of the world's finest collections of antiquities, covering the
period from the early Bronze
Age in the Greek territories
(c. 3,200 BC) to the establishment
of Christianity in the Roman
Empire (AD 313). Among the oldest pieces are Cycladic marble
figurines and the first known
signed Sophilos bowl and stand,
with black figures (Greece,
c. 580 BC). The **[A] Elgin Marbles**
(5th century BC) depicting the
birth of Athena amongst other

a/s/e London

British Museum
Ground Floor
(Rooms 1–35)

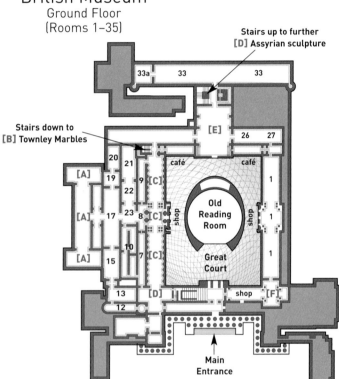

Stairs up to further
[D] Assyrian sculpture

Stairs down to
[B] Townley Marbles

33a   33   33

[E]

26   27

café   café

20
21
[A]
19
9   [C]
Old
Reading
Room
1

22
[A]
17
23   [C]
8
shop
shop
1

10
[A]
15
7   [C]
Great
Court
1

13   [D]
shop   [F]

12

Main
Entrance

[A] Elgin Marbles (room 18)   [E] Hoa Hakananai'a statue
[B] Townley Marbles (room 84)   (room 24)
[C] Rosetta Stone (room 4)   [F] Mildenhall Treasure
[D] Assyrian sculpture   (room 2 temporarily)
    (rooms 6, 7, 52–57)

scenes, were considered the pinnacle of Greek sculpture in 1816 when they were removed by Lord Elgin from the Temple of Athena Parthenos on the Acropolis in Athens. The *Discobolus*, antiquity's athletic ideal copied from a 5th-century BC Greek bronze, is one of several outstanding pieces of classical Roman sculpture known as the **[B]** **Townley Marbles**, excavated from Hadrian's Villa, Tivoli, by Charles Townley. He began collecting whilst on a Grand Tour in 1768 and displayed his findings at his home in Westminster, where they quickly became a revered attraction and consequently influenced British artistic taste at that time.

Ancient Egypt and Sudan (*rooms 4 & 61–66*): Exhibits span the cultures of the Nile Valley from the Neolithic period (c. 10th century BC), through the Pharaonic period, to the Coptic era (12th century AD). Exhibits range from small funerary and domestic items to temple architecture. The **[C]** **Rosetta Stone** (196 BC) arrived at the museum in 1802. Inscriptions in hieroglyphic, demotic Egyptian and Greek proved to be hugely significant for Egyptology when Jean-François Champollion cracked

the Stone's code in 1822 and revealed the previously 'lost' ancient civilization of Egypt. The colossal bust of Rameses II from Thebes was the first major piece to enter the collection. Exhibits of papyri include the Book of the Dead of Any, considered the best illustrated papyrus in existence. Mummy cases are displayed alongside X-rays and CAT scans revealing objects beneath the wrappings.

Ancient Near East (*rooms 6–10, 34 & 52–59*): A wealth of objects from the ancient civilizations of Mesopotamia (Iraq), Iran, the Levant, Anatolia and Arabia, from Neolithic times to the 7th century AD. Outstanding **[D]** **Assyrian sculpture** includes the Black Obelisk of Shalmaneser III from Nimrud (858–824 BC) glorifying the achievements of the king, relief carvings from the Palace of Sennarcherib at Ninevah, and massive human-headed winged bulls (710–105 BC), each weighing 16 tons, from Sargon II's palace at Khorsabad. Among clay cuneiform tablets is the Flood Tablet, a Babylonian version of the Biblical deluge, which enthralled Victorian visitors. The Oxus Treasure (4th–5th centuries BC), is a sophisticated

a/s/e London

hoard of gold and silver from the Achaemenid Persian Empire.

Africa, Oceania and the Americas (*rooms 24, 26, 27 & 25*): Among the ethnographic collections are a rare Hohao spirit board, from Papua New Guinea representing a human figure, thought to bring success to hunters. The monumental Easter Island statue, [E] **Hoa Hakananai'a**, at just over four metres high and weighing four tons, was brought to England in 1868 on the survey ship *HMS Topaze*. The Mixtec-Aztec turquoise mosaics, including the double-headed serpent, or *coatl*, were possibly presented to conquistador Hernando Cortés in 1519. The Africa Galleries contain the bronze head of a Yoruba ruler (12th–14th century).

Prehistory and Archaeology of Europe (*rooms 41–51*): A remarkable collection of important British discoveries. Among them are the elaborately wrought gold, silver and bronze hoard of Snettisham Torc (c. 75 BC) from Norfolk. The [F] **Mildenhall Treasure** of Roman silver tableware from Suffolk was discovered in the 1930s by a farmer. The ship-burial of an

A double-headed serpent from the Mixtec-Aztec collection at the British Museum

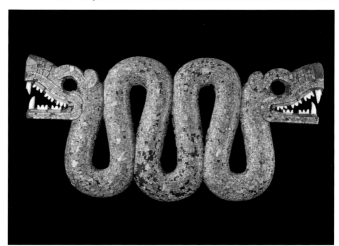

East-Anglian king (c. AD 625–630), excavated at Sutton Hoo, Suffolk, in 1939, was one of the greatest archaeological discoveries in Britain, revealing elaborate jewellery and weapons which changed earlier perceptions of a primitive Anglo Saxon society.

Prints and Drawings (*room 90*): This vast collection has over 50,000 drawings and some two million prints from the 15th century to the present. In 1895, the Malcolm collection alone provided the British Museum with over 1,000 Old Master pieces, including 138 drawings by Albrecht Dürer, and Michelangelo's studies for the Sistine Chapel.

Coins and Medals (*room 68*): This collection is unrivalled due to the British Museum's ongoing legal responsibility to process 'treasure' found in England and Wales. To date, the collection boasts almost a million objects, including coins from 7th century BC, paper money from 14th-century China, and an exceptional collection of commemorative medals. Some 9,000 are displayed in special thematic exhibitions.

Asia (*rooms 33, 67 & 91–94*): This department shows objects covering the period c. 4,000 BCE

to the present. Among the most revered treasures of the British Museum are intricately carved 1st–3rd century limestone reliefs from the Great Stupa at Amaravati, southeast India, and the supremely graceful 9th-century cast bronze Bodhisattva Tara from Sri Lanka, given to the museum by the Governor of Ceylon in 1830. Jade, highly-prized for centuries in China, is represented by a Hongshun period coiled dragon (c. 3500 BC), and Ming Dynasty carved belt plaques (16th–17th century). Among the great variety of Chinese paintings is the remarkable group of illustrations (AD 618–960) from the Valley of a Thousand Buddhas, Dunhuang. Sophisticated Chinese ceramics include the white porcelain Phoenix-headed ewer (9th–11th century). The Japanese collection of graphic art has examples of 17th–19th century Ukiyo-e prints and paintings, and woodblock prints of the Edo period (1600–1868) by Hokusai. There is also a unique collection of Korean art, including its masterpiece, the 17th-century Moon Jar, one of only 20 remaining in the world. A range of Islamic pottery includes Iznik ceramics from Turkey.

National Gallery

Open: Thur–Tues 10–6, Wed 10–9; closed 1 Jan, 24–26 Dec
Charges: Free entry, except special exhibitions **Tel:** 020 7747 2885
Web: www.nationalgallery.org.uk **Underground:** Charing Cross,
Leicester Square **Map:** p. 67, C5–C6
Highlights: *The Ambassadors* by Hans Holbein the Younger; *The Arnolfini Portrait* by Jan van Eyck; *Bathers at Asnières* by Georges Seurat; *The Battle of San Romano* by Paolo Uccello; *'The Rokeby Venus'* by Diego Velazquez; *The Wilton Diptych* (unknown artist)

The National Gallery's collection of Western European art (1250–1900) is greatly revered and exceptionally beautiful. (Tate Britain is the official home of British art; *see p. 101*). Its home is the familiar porticoed building (1833–38) designed by William Wilkins, on Trafalgar Square. The collection, established from 1824, had grown to such an extent by the 1950s that extra space was vital and in 1985 the Sainsbury family offered to sponsor a new wing. The initial plan, denounced by Prince Charles as a 'monstrous carbuncle', was replaced by Robert Venturi's design, and the Sainsbury Wing, which wittily echoes the classicism of the Wilkins building, opened in 1991. The National Gallery's restaurant, The National Dining Rooms, is recommended (*see p. 91*). There is so much on view in the National Gallery that only the highlights are detailed here, chronologically, beginning in the Sainsbury Wing:

1250–1500 (*Sainsbury Wing, Level 2, rooms 51–66*): Elegant, pale grey galleries set off stately Italian *quattrocento* paintings and Gothic works from Germany and the Netherlands. Falling outside these categories, but shown alongside them, is **[A] The Wilton Diptych** (c. 1395), in room 53. It is an exceptional devotional work from Wilton House in Wiltshire, seat of the Earls of Pembroke, possibly originating in France. Against a gold background Richard II is presented by his patron saints to the Virgin and Child, in heavenly blue, seated before a choir of angels.

National Gallery

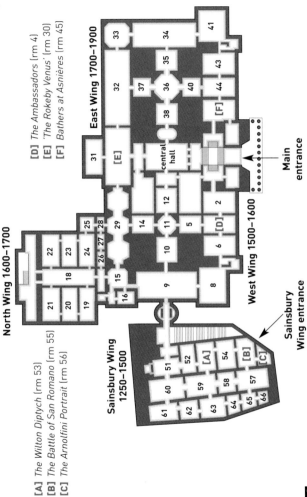

East Wing 1700–1900

North Wing 1600–1700

West Wing 1500–1600

Sainsbury Wing 1250–1500

central hall

Main entrance

Sainsbury Wing entrance

[D] *The Ambassadors* (rm 4)
[E] *'The Rokeby Venus'* (rm 30)
[F] *Bathers at Asnières* (rm 45)

[A] *The Wilton Diptych* (rm 53)
[B] *The Battle of San Romano* (rm 55)
[C] *The Arnolfini Portrait* (rm 56)

Italy: The earliest work here is Margarito of Arezzo's *Virgin and Child* (1260s), which recalls Byzantine icons. Giotto, however, shows a shift towards more supple figures in *Pentecost* (c. 1306–12). Paolo Uccello's meticulously executed **[B]** *The Battle of San Romano* (mid-15th century) reveals his interest in perspective. Botticelli's *Mystic Nativity* (1500) is delicate and joyful, while two versions of *The Agony in the Garden* by Venetian artists Andrea Mantegna and Giovanni Bellini, in the 1460s, make an interesting comparison. Portraits after Bellini's imperious *Doge Leonardo Loredan* (1501–04) in a sumptuous robe, and Antonello da Messina's masterful *Portrait of a Man* (1475). Room 66 is dedicated to masterpieces by Piero della Francesca. *The Baptism of Christ* (1450s), painted for the church of Sansepolcro, Piero's home, is typical of his dignified and thoughtful creativity.

Netherlands and Germany: The technique of oil painting probably originated in the Netherlands and was used to brilliant effect by Jan van Eyck in **[C]** *The Arnolfini Portrait* (1434) to convey textures and surfaces, particularly shown on the brass chandelier.

1500–1600 (*West Wing, rooms 2–14*) **Italy:** Incredibly rich pickings of Renaissance art bring together preoccupations with light, perspective, anatomy and composition in both religious and mythological subjects. In Leonardo da Vinci's atmospheric altarpiece *The Virgin of the Rocks* (c. 1491), Mary tenderly supports the kneeling Christ Child who blesses John the Baptist. In Room 8 are Michelangelo's unfinished version of the *Entombment* (c. 1500), Raphael's eloquent *Mond Crucifixion* (1502–3), and the strikingly lifelike portrait of Pope Julius II (1511). *An Allegory* (c. 1550) is a sensual portrayal of a nude Venus embraced by Cupid painted by Agnolo Bronzino as a gift for Francis I of France. There are lush Venetian works by Veronese and Tintoretto, and the resplendent Central Hall is dominated by Titian's stately *Vendramin Family* (mid-1540s) who venerate a cross.

Netherlands: *The Virgin and Child with Saints and Donor* (c. 1510) by Gerard David stands out from the other exhibits, as does the deformed but elegantly clothed *Grotesque Old Woman* (c. 1525) by Quentin Massys.

Germany: Exceptional among German sixteenth-century paintings is **[D]** *The Ambassadors* (1533) by Hans Holbein the Younger, depicting Jean de Dinteville, French Ambassador at the Court of Henry VIII, surrounded by paraphernalia representing Humanist learning and coded messages. The puzzling foreground shape turns out to be a skull, symbol of mortality, when viewed from the right.

1600–1700 (*North Wing, rooms 15–32*) **Dutch works:**
Characteristic of domestic interiors are Pieter de Hooch's *Courtyard of a House in Delft* (1658), and Vermeer's *A Young Woman Standing at a Virginal* (c. 1670), virtuosos of detail, perspective and light. Dutch artists, most notably Albert Cuyp and Jacob van Ruisdael, elevated nature and landscape to the role of major subject. Several outstanding works by Rembrandt include *Woman Taken in Adultery* (1644) and *Belshazzar's Feast* (c. 1635).

Flemish works: This section is dominated by the large Baroque *Peace and War* (1629–30) by Rubens, worked on when he was in England as diplomatic envoy to Philip IV of Spain, and the enchanting *Chapeau de Paille* (c. 1622) of a young girl in a large hat. Van Dyck painted the hugely flattering *Equestrian Portrait of Charles I* (c. 1637–38) shortly before the Civil War.

Italy: Included here is *Supper at Emmaus* (1601) by Caravaggio, a work of heightened tension and drama—note the finely-balanced bowl of fruit.

France: Artists Nicholas Poussin and Claude Lorrain (rooms 19–20) had differing approaches to landscape. Poussin favoured classical themes, learned in Rome, and rigorous figure compositions, as in *A Bacchanalian Revel before a Term* (1632–33). Claude typically created atmosphere and depth in works such as *Landscape with Hagar and the Angel* (1646). He was greatly admired by the English artist Turner, who insisted that two of his own canvases be hung alongside Claude's (room 15).

Spain: Works in room 30 are dominated by religious scenes or court paintings by El Greco and Murillo, the exception being the dispassionate and exquisite **[E]** '*The Rokeby Venus*' (1647–51), the only existing female nude by court painter, Velazquez.

1700–1900 (*East Wing, rooms 33–46*): Representative of the 18th century are works by the

a/s/e London

The Fighting Temeraire (1839) by J.M.W. Turner at the National Gallery

Italian, Canaletto, and from Spain, a vibrant portrait by Goya of *Doña Isabel de Porcel* (before 1805).

Britain: Works include fluent portraits by Thomas Lawrence and Gainsborough. Evocative of the Industrial Revolution are the demise of a great sailing ship, *The Fighting Temeraire* (1839; *pictured above*), and the arrival of the railway, *Rain, Steam and Speed* (before 1844) recorded by Turner. Quintessentially English

are Hogarth's *Marriage à la Mode* (c. 1743), and Constable's *The Hay Wain* (1821).

France: Key paintings include Manet's *Music in the Tuileries Gardens* (1862), Monet's *The Thames below Westminster* (1871) and Renoir's *Boating on the Seine* (1875). Other major works are Seurat's monumental [F] *Bathers at Asnières* (1884), Cézanne's *Les Grandes Baigneuses*, and one version of van Gogh's *Sunflowers* (1888).

National Portrait Gallery

Open: Sat–Wed 10–6, Thur–Fri 10–9; closed 24–26 Dec
Charges: Free entry, except special exhibitions **Tel:** 020 7312 2463
Web: www.npg.org.uk **Underground:** Charing Cross, Leicester
Square **Map:** p. 67, C5–C6
Highlights: *Elizabeth I* by Marcus Gheeraerts the Younger; *Ellen Terry* by G.F. Watts; *Henry VIII* by Hans Holbein the Younger; *Self portrait* by Patrick Heron

The National Portrait Gallery, established in 1856, pioneered the singular objective of presenting great figures in British history to the nation. The collection is inspirational and keeps up to date with modern public figures. The Primary Collection of 10,000 paintings, drawings, sculptures, engravings and photographs, includes portraits from Shakespeare to J. K. Rowling. The Portrait Restaurant on the 3rd floor is recommended (*see p. 91*).

Tudor and Stuart Collection, 16th–17th century (*2nd floor, rooms 1–8*): This period features mainly royalty and nobility, most of them male. The earliest surviving portrait is Henry VII from 1505. The cartoon of **Henry VIII** (c. 1536) by Holbein for the lost mural in Whitehall Palace, on which all later portraits of the king were based, is one of the most important works in the gallery. The timeless image of **Elizabeth I** (c. 1592) by Marcus Gheeraerts the Younger, was painted during her stay in Ditchley, Oxfordshire, and shows her full length in a sumptuous gown, standing serenely on a globe while tempestuous weather rages behind her. Her favourite, the Earl of Leicester, as well as Francis Drake, and Walter Raleigh are also represented. Stuart dynasty portraits show off the beautiful costumes of the period. Van Dyck, official painter to Charles I, painted Lord George Stuart, Seigneur d'Aubigny (c. 1638), a royalist killed in battle.

18th-century Collection (*2nd floor, rooms 9–14*): During the Hanoverian period of the Enlightenment, portraits of public

a/s/e London

figures increased. Among them are architect, Sir Christopher Wren (1711; *pictured opposite*) by Godfrey Kneller, and a terra-cotta bust of the painter William Hogarth (c. 1741) by Roubiliac.

Regency period (*2nd floor, rooms 17–20*): The Prince Regent, crowned as George IV in 1820, is depicted in an oil sketch by Thomas Lawrence. Famous figures of the day include military and naval heroes the Duke of Wellington and Admiral Nelson, as well as Romantic poets and novelists such as Byron, Keats, and Wordsworth. Jane Austen is delicately sketched by her sister.

Victorian Collection (*1st floor, rooms 21–29*): Symbolic of the Victorian concept of the Empire is Thomas Jones Barker's *The Secret of England's Greatness* (c. 1863) in which Queen Victoria presents a Bible to an African convert received at Windsor. In contrast is James Tissot's suave *Fredick Gustavus Burnaby* (1870), cavalry officer and explorer. Writers include Dickens, Thackeray, George Eliot, and the three Brontë sisters, and the artist Edwin Landseer, dwarfed by the lions he is modelling for Trafalgar Square c. 1865 (*see p. 87*). 'Hall of Fame'

by G.F. Watts is a series of portraits of powerful, visionary men such as Thomas Carlyle (who described his portrait as 'insufferable') and William Morris. There is also a sensuous portrait of the actress **Ellen Terry**, who was briefly married to Watts.

20th-century collection (*1st floor, rooms 30–32*): Here are suffragette Emmeline Pankhurst, and James Guthrie's *Statesmen of World War I* (1924–30) which shows Prime Ministers Asquith, Lloyd George and Churchill, among others, below *Winged Victory* in the Louvre. The *Conversation Piece at the Royal Lodge, Windsor* (1950) is a nostalgic record by James Gunn of George VI, Queen Elizabeth and the Princesses Elizabeth and Margaret taking tea. Splendid portraits by, and of, the Bloomsbury Group include Virginia Woolf by her sister, Vanessa Bell. Of the self-portraits, those by **Patrick Heron** and Maggi Hambling are striking. On the first-floor landing are likenesses of the present royal family. Selections from the important collection of photography from the 1840s onwards are shown throughout the displays.

Sir Christopher Wren (1711) at the National Portrait Gallery

SIR CHR: WREN.
Late Surveyor General of
the Royal Buildings.
He died the 25th of Feb. 1723, aged 91.

Wallace Collection

Open: Daily 10–5, closed 24–26 Dec **Charges:** Free entry
Tel: 020 7563 9500 **Web:** www.wallacecollection.org **Underground:**
Baker Street, Bond Street **Map:** p. 66, B2
Highlights: Armouries collection; *Celebrating the Birth* by Jan
Steen; furniture by André-Charles Boulle; *The Laughing Cavalier* by
Frans Hals; *Madame de Pompadour* by François Boucher; *The Swing*
by Jean-Honoré Fragonard

This is a charming museum, in the former residence of the Richard
Seymour-Conway family, Marquesses of Hertford. It contains a stunning display of predominantly 18th-century French painting, decorative arts and a rare collection of arms and armour. The collections
were arranged mainly by the 4th Marquess and his son, Richard
Wallace, both of whom spent much of their lives in Paris. The house
and contents were opened to the public in 1900.

Ground floor
In the Hall is the sentimental but exquisitely executed horse 'portrait', *The
Arab Tent* (c. 1865) by Edwin Landseer, best-selling English painter of the
day. Superb examples of French Rococo decorative arts in the Back State
Room include a gilt bronze chandelier by Caffieri and a Sèvres porcelain
inkstand by J.-C. Duplessis, gifts from Louis XV to his daughters. **Furniture
by André-Charles Boulle** in the Billiard and Dining Rooms is representative
of the best of French 17th–18th-century works, for instance the magnificent Cabinet (c. 1665–70) of oak and ebony, rich marquetry and lacquer.
The **Armouries collection** is second only to the Royal Armoury at the Tower
of London (*see p. 51*). Many magnificent examples were acquired by Sir
Richard from French and English collections. A choice example of Oriental
Armoury is the 17th century Indian dagger with a solid gold hilt set with
diamonds, rubies and emeralds. European Armoury ranges from swords
used by the Crusader knights to a decorative late-15th-century German
tournament shield, as well as a rare example of equestrian armour for
horse and rider, c. 1575–85, made in southern Germany.

First floor

A grand white-marble staircase with a magnificent balustrade sold off for scrap by the Palais Mazarin, Paris, sweeps up to the first-floor galleries. On the stairs and landing are four stunning paintings (1752–53) by François Boucher, showing Apollo rising from the river Oceana to journey across the heavens, before sinking back below the waves. The Oval and Large Drawing Rooms, once used as ballrooms, contain Jean-Honoré Fragonard's most delectable work, **The Swing** (1767), the very epitome of Rococo grace, levity and eroticism with a brilliant mastery of landscape and atmosphere. Boucher's more decorous but equally delicious **Madame de Pompadour** (1759), whose arm rests on a statue of *Friendship consoling Love*, refers to the state of her relationship with Louis XV. Another example of intricate Boulle workmanship is the wardrobe (c. 1700) of oak and ebony with exquisite examples of *première* and *contre-partie* marquetry in a variety of materials. The Small Drawing Room contains objects such as the elegant perfume burner that once belonged to Marie-Antoinette. Eighteenth-century paintings in the Boudoir and the Study include *The Strawberry Girl* (1770s) by Joshua Reynolds, and Elisabeth Vigée le Brun's lively portrait of *Madame Perregaux* (1789). The East Drawing Room and Galleries I–III display Dutch and Flemish 17th-century pictures including *Self-portrait in a Black Cap* (c. 1637) by a young Rembrandt. Anecdotal works loaded with ribald clues point to the licentious demeanour of the old man in Jan Steen's *Harpsichord Lesson* (late 1660s), and the dubious siring of a baby in **Celebrating the Birth** (1664). The Great Gallery contains an array of key works by leading European artists of the period, including Rubens, Poussin, Gainsborough, Velázquez and Murillo. But the best known is undoubtedly **The Laughing Cavalier** (1624) by Frans Hals. This magnificent portrait of an unidentified gallant with an ambiguous expression, wearing sumptuous clothes covered with symbols of love's vacillations, was possibly a betrothal portrait. The West Gallery and Room provides an opportunity to compare the relative merits of views of Venice by Canaletto and Guardi alongside 18th-century Italian furniture and a range of miniatures.

There is a charming and very popular restaurant (*see p. 91*) in the covered courtyard.

London

a/s/e

Courtauld Gallery & Somerset House

Open: Daily 10–6, last admission 5.30, limited openings 24 & 31 Dec & 1 Jan; closed 25–26 Dec **Charges:** Entry charge, except 1st Mon of month 10–2 **Tel:** 020 7848 2526 **Web:** www.courtauld.ac.uk **Underground:** Covent Garden, Temple **Map:** p. 67, C7 **Highlights:** *A Bar at the Folies-Bergère* by Edouard Manet; *The Exhibition Stare-case* by Thomas Rowlandson; *Montagne Sainte-Victoire* by Paul Cézanne; *Theatre Box* by Auguste Renoir

Somerset House (1776–1801) was the masterpiece of William Chambers, once architectural tutor to George III and head of the King's Office of Works. It is entered via the elegant Doric vestibule decorated with busts of worthies such as Michelangelo and Isaac Newton. These are relevant to the learned societies and government offices for which the building was intended, and surround a large, handsome courtyard with façades enriched with sculptures by leading Academicians. A 55-jet fountain was installed in 2000, which transforms into a skating rink in winter.

Initially the home of the Royal Academy of Arts (*see p. 110*), Somerset House now hosts the Courtauld Gallery, a series of private collections on the first and second floors of the Strand block. The 'Fine Rooms' on the first floor, with ornamented plasterwork and painted ceilings, include the Antique Academy decorated with the initials of the Royal Academy. From here, a narrow staircase continues up to the second floor, satirised in **The Exhibition Stare-case** (c. 1800) by Thomas Rowlandson, to the Royal Academy Great Room where the Summer Exhibitions took place from 1780 to 1836.

The main attraction is the stunning Impressionist and Post-Impressionist collection endowed by the textile magnate, Samuel Courtauld, and which used to adorn his residence, Home House, nearby in Portman Square. The brilliant 20th-century works include Fauve paintings by Matisse, Derain and Dufy, and examples of

Thomas Gainsborough's portrait of his wife (c. 1779), displayed at the Courtauld Gallery

German Expressionism, including works by Kandinsky, as well as Kokoschka's large *Prometheus Triptych* (1950). British 20th century art is well represented by Bloomsbury Group artists Vanessa Bell, Duncan Grant and Roger Fry, and by later artists such as Ben Nicholson and Ivor Hitchens. Many world-famous French Impressionist and Post-Impressionist images reside here including Manet's enigmatic *A Bar at the Folies-Bergère* (1881–82), *Two Dancers on a Stage* (c. 1874) by Dégas, and Renoir's *The Theatre Box* (*La Loge*; 1874). Landscapes include Cézanne's **Montagne Sainte-Victoire** (1885–87) and Monet's *Antibes* (1888). Cézanne's range and brilliance can also be seen in *Card Players* (1892–95) and *Still Life with Plaster Cast* (1894). By Gauguin are two Polynesian paintings of 1897, *Never More* and *Te Rerioa*.

Eighteenth-century painting includes Thomas Gainsborough's portrait of his wife (*pictured above*), a full-length male portrait by Goya, and a rich group of oil sketches by Tiepolo. Representing the 17th century are religious works and landscapes by Rubens and his charming portrait of the *Family of Jan Breugel the Elder* (1612–13). Renaissance works include an altarpiece by Botticelli and *Adam and Eve* (1526) by Cranach the Elder. The Courtauld also holds a major sculpture collection with Renaissance bas-reliefs, and works by Dégas, Frank Dobson, Henry Moore and Rodin. Rare prints and drawings, from the Renaissance to the 20th century, are exhibited in rotation and decorative arts are represented throughout the galleries.

in the area

British Library (*exhibition galleries and shop open Mon & Wed–Fri 9.30–6, Tues 9.30–8, Sat 9.30–5, Sun & hols 11–5; for entry to the Reading Rooms check on-line, free entry, Web: www.bl.uk, Underground: Euston, King's Cross*). Having moved from the British Museum (*see p. 69*) in 1998, the British Library continues in its quest to collect every printed text published in the United Kingdom. Already, the collection consists of 150 million items in most known languages. Regular exhibitions (and the reading rooms) make available such fascinating pieces as the ancient charter of liberties, the Magna Carta; the *Times* newspaper first edition from 1788; music manuscripts by the Beatles; and the recording of Nelson Mandela's trial speech. **Off map p. 67, A6**

Photographers' Gallery (*open Mon–Wed, Fri & Sat 11–6, Thur 11–8, Sun 12–6, free entry, Tel: 020 7831 1772, Web: www.photonet.org.uk, Underground: Leicester Square*). One of the first independent galleries in the UK devoted to photography, showcasing the work of up-and-coming photographers. It also awards the annual Citibank Photography Prize. Contemporary British prints, including signed limited editions, are on sale in the print sales gallery; the gallery's bookshop is one of the best in the UK. The gallery will move to Soho in 2010. **Map p. 67, C6**

Sir John Soane's Museum (*open Tues–Sat 10–5, 1st Tues in month also 6pm–9pm, closed Sun, Mon & hols, free entry, Tel: 020 7405 2107, Web: www.soane.org, Underground: Holborn*). The distinctive British architect, Sir John Soane, is represented in this most unusual museum containing his lifetime collection of antiquities, marbles, plaster casts, paintings, drawings and books (*pictured right*). Its inauguration in March 1825 was attended by 850 guests, among them Turner, Coleridge and Robert Peel. The rooms are intensely crowded, but Soane carefully positioned mirrors and incorporated unusual views, changes of level, and overhead skylights to set off the exhibits to best advantage. Among remarkable pieces are the alabaster sarcophagus of the Pharaoh Seti I, the antique Greek 'Cawdor Vase', plaster casts of the *Apollo Belvedere* and Medici *Venus*, and hosts of pictures including Hogarth's series *Rake's Progress* and Piranesi's views of Paestum. There are also plaster models by Neoclassical sculptor John Flaxman, and architectural fragments from Inigo Jones's Banqueting House and the old Palace of Westminster. **Map p. 67, B7**

Trafalgar Square

(*Underground: Charing Cross*). London's most animated open space, named after the English victory at the battle of Trafalgar (off Portugal) in 1805. The 5m-statue of the hero of Trafalgar, Admiral Horatio Nelson, sculpted by E.H. Baily, stands atop the 50m Nelson Column erected 1839–42. At the base are bronze reliefs showing Nelson's other victories, and around it are large, benevolent lions, designed by Edwin Landseer in the 1860s. The corner plinths bear an eques-

Sir John Soane's antiquities collection is on show at his home, now a museum

trian statue of George IV by Francis Chantrey (1834), and virtually forgotten military heroes, Charles Napier by George Canon Adams (1855) and Henry Havelock by William Behnes (1861). The extra northwest plinth places modern sculptures in rotation; a controversial but exciting policy. In November 2007, Thomas Schütte's layers of translucent red, blue and yellow glass, *Model for a Hotel 2007*, was installed. Models for the next work have been submitted by Jeremy Deller, Tracey Emin, Antony Gormley, Anish Kapoor, Yinka Shonibare and Bob and Roberta Smith (their submissions are on display at the National Gallery; *see p. 74*). The oldest building overlooking the square is the church of St Martin-in-the-Fields (1722–26), where Nell Gwyn, Thomas Chippendale, Joshua Reynolds and William Hogarth, among others, are buried. Whitehall, lined with government offices and containing the Cenotaph (1919–20) by Edwin Lutyens, exits to the south. **Map p. 67, C5–C6**

eat

You will have trouble walking more than a few metres without coming across a top-class, unusual or tempting eating venue in the West End of London. Old established restaurants with old established etiquette, such as Rules, compete for space with high quality relative newcomers such as L'Atelier de Joel Robuchon. Equally at home here are restaurants representing food from every continent such as Sardo serving a Sardinian menu, and pubs and cafés serving truly British food. Then there are the world-renowned galleries—National Gallery, National Portrait Gallery and the Wallace Collection—with equally excellent restaurants. It really is a case of how many meals you can fit in during one day. For price categories, see p. 11; all restaurants are located on map pp. 66 & 67.

1 £££ L'Atelier de Joel Robuchon, *13–15 West Street, Tel: 020 7010 8600, open Mon–Sat, 12.30–3 & 5.30-midnight; Sun 12.30–3 & 5.30-10.30, Underground: Covent Garden, Leicester Square.* Based on his successful Parisian formula of carefully crafted small *dégustation* dishes, maestro Robuchon has set up a three-floor 'studio' in London. Downstairs is ultra-serious dining, where the fastidious work of the kitchen is in full view. Among the array of small tasters which contribute to this pleasurable experience are Pig's trotter on parmesan toast, Scallop with seaweed butter, tiny Beef and foie gras burgers, and Truffle mashed potato. On the floor above is the less formal La Cuisine, and at the top is a bar.

2 £££ Hakkasan, *8 Hanway Place, Tel: 020 7927 7000, open Mon–Fri 12–3 & 6–12; Sat 12–4 & 6–12; Sun 12–4 & 6–11, Underground: Tottenham Court Road.* Ultra select, despite the unpromising entrance, at Hakkasan you can drink *sakétinis* and eat exquisite Asian dishes. The setting is dark latticed screens and subdued lighting and the ingenious cooking uses luxury ingredients for dishes such as Sea bass cooked with sliced pork and Chinese sausage and shitake mushroom cooked in a lotus leaf. Beware the two-hour turn around. A high is dim-sum, served at midday only.

3 £££ Rules, *35 Maiden Lane, Tel: 020 7836 5314, open Mon–Sat 12–11.30, Sun 12–10.30, Underground: Covent Garden.* ■ Reputedly the oldest restaurant in

London and bastion of British cooking, Rules cannot be left out. Its charming old-world décor, the historic list of former diners, and its tradition for serving game (in season) make it a sought-after address. Dedicated to British products, it even has its own estate in the Pennines. The beautifully cooked traditional dishes and produce include Devon crab & lobster bisque, followed by Steak & kidney pudding; then comes great British Stilton and Upside-down apple tart. Also in good English tradition, the wines are mainly French.

4 ££ Andrew Edmunds, *46 Lexington Street, Tel: 020 7437 5708, open Mon–Fri 12.30-3 & 6-10.45; Sat 1-3 & 6-10.45; Sun 1-3.30 & 6-10.30, Underground: Oxford Street, Piccadilly Circus.* ■ Wine aficionado, Edmunds's snug restaurant on two floors at the heart of Soho is justifiably a popular place—it's important to book a week in advance. The seasonable food is beautifully but unfussily cooked. Down to earth at midday, it becomes more romantic in the evening. Good flavours and excellent wine selection.

5 ££ Axis Restaurant, *1 Aldwych, Tel: 020 7300 0300, open Mon–Fri 12-2.30 & 5.45-10.45, Sat 5.45-11.30, Underground: Covent Garden, Temple.* The refurbished Axis Restaurant, part of the One Aldwych hotel (*see p. 14*), flies the British flag. Its scrupulously sourced ingredients and modern takes on such traditional treats include Smoked eel, venison, rump

Sphère de sucre à la violette et litchi, glace au lait at L'Atelier de Joel Robuchon

London

a/s/e

and kidney of Herwick lamb, and Steamed treacle sponge. The hugely popular Lobby Bar with stunning flower arrangements, tall windows, high ceilings, and exciting modern art works, has a vast range of champagnes, wines and beers, not to mention 63 cocktails.

⑥ ££ Sardo, *45 Grafton Way, Tel: 020 7387 2521, open Mon–Fri 12–3 & 6–11; Sat 6–11, Underground: Warren Street*. A low-key setting specialising in outstanding Sardinian cooking and wine. Succulent olives, aromatic breads, cured tuna, mutton prosciutto, or baby squid start you off, followed by skilfull pasta dishes or grilled meat and fish. To complete the meal are classic desserts such as Tiramisu or Sebada, a pastry with orange peel and cheese.

⑦ ££ La Trouvaille, *12a Newburgh Street, Tel: 020 7287 8488, open Mon–Fri 12–3 & 6–11, closed Sat lunch and Sun all day, Underground: Oxford Circus*. As authentic as a French *bistrot* can get—both for food and ambiance—this is indeed quite a find. On the menu are terrine, *escargots*, veal, beef with seasonal vegetables, and *fondant au chocolat*. There are also snacks at the bar.

⑧ £ Barrafina, *54 Frith Street, Tel: 020 7813 8016 (no reservations), open Mon–Sat 12–3 & 5–11, Underground: Tottenham Court Road*. A tiny informal tapas bar with Spanish and Portuguese dishes designed, as in Spain, not to linger over. *Tortilla*, suckling pig, *chiperones*, and all the favourites, are

beautifully cooked and ingredients carefully sourced to accompany a good glass of sherry.

⑨ £ La Fromagerie, *2–6 Moxon Street, Tel: 020 7935 0341, open Mon 10.30–7.30, Tues–Fri 8–7.30, Sat 9–7, Sun 10–6, Underground: Baker Street, Bond Street*. A must for cheese lovers. The Tasting Café serves simple but quality fare. Spanish breakfast comprises of cured hams, *manchego* and crusty bread; lunch consists of two menus—traditional La Fromagerie products, or the Kitchen Menu with soups, salads and stews. Teatime treats tempt with a changing selection of cakes and pastries and Valrhona hot chocolate.

⑩ £ The Kerala, *15 Great Castle Street, Tel: 020 7580 2125, open daily 12–3 & 5.30–11, Underground: Oxford Circus*. ▬ This restaurant rates highly for its Southern Indian cooking and amazingly good-value lunch buffet menu. *Dosas*, seafood dishes, and curries—whether simple or more complex, the food is fragrant and delicious.

④ £ Mildred's, *45 Lexington Street, Tel: 020 7494 1634 (no reservations), open Mon–Sat, midday–11, Underground: Piccadilly Circus*. Next door to Andrew Edmonds, Mildred's is something of an institution. Outside is a blue-painted shopfront, inside are white walls, red banquettes and a bar to wait for an opportunity to squeeze in. Wholesome, imaginative and inexpensive, the wide range of organic and vegetarian choices includes good veggie burgers, chunky chips, flat bread, salads, *crostini*, or more elaborate dishes, as well as daily specials and takeaway.

11 £ Museum Tavern, *49 Great Russell Street, Tel: 020 7242 8987, open Mon–Sat 11–11, Sun 12–10.30,* *Underground: Russell Square, Tottenham Court Road.* On the doorstep of the British Museum, the traditional real ales on tap make this pub worth visiting; try a pint of Theakston's Old Peculiar or St Austell Tribute.

Eating in the Galleries

The V&A museum, under its pioneering director Henry Cole, was the first in the world to provide a restaurant for visitors in the 19th century. Since then, each of London's top galleries has invested in their own restaurant with top chefs, innovative menus and the best settings in the capital.

£££ The Wallace Restaurant, in the courtyard of the Wallace Collection (*see p. 82 for information*). In keeping with the collection, this elegant, covered courtyard restaurant is a modern take on a French brasserie with fairly elaborate and prettily presented dishes. Seafood, oysters and caviar appear frequently. For the gourmands there are patisseries and ice-cream at all times. It's essential to reserve at lunchtime. **Map p. 66, B2**

££ The National Dining Rooms, in the Sainsbury Wing at the National Gallery (*see p. 74 for information*). The National joined the list of best places to eat in 2007 under Oliver Peyton's watchful eye. Now you can enjoy beautiful British food including crab cakes, Suffolk asparagus, or eight varieties of tomato, and a varied bakery selection. **Map p. 67, C5–C6**

££ The Portrait Restaurant, on the 3rd floor of the National Portrait Gallery (*see p. 79 for information*). ■ This modern bar and restaurant is popular (and important to book) for the unique views of Admiral Nelson on his column in Trafalgar Square, as well as the food. Lunch is a serious affair with dishes such as Baked whole black bream, or Scottish venison Wellington. **Map p. 67, C5–C6**

shop

The West End is the shoppers' Mecca. Some 200 million visitors a year make the pilgrimage to the 300 shops and almost two million square metres of retail space along the hectic one-and-a-half mile stretch of Oxford Street between Oxford Circus and Marble Arch. But if you can't stand the pace, alternatives include the elite St Christopher's Place and Marylebone High Street, elegant Regent Street, and revived Carnaby Street, as well as all-singing-all-dancing Covent Garden. All shops are located on map pp. 66 & 67, and are generally open Mon–Sat 10–6 or 7, Sun 12–6, with late night opening on Thursdays.

OXFORD STREET

A Selfridges, *400 Oxford Street, Tel: 0870 837 7377, Underground: Bond Street, Marble Arch.* Established by American, Gordon Selfridge, who brought the department store idea to Europe, this was the first department store on Oxford Street, arriving in 1909. Its familiar façade, with giant Ionic columns and the 3.3m-high sculpture, Queen of the Clock, dominates this section of Oxford Street. The window-dressing is a major feature. Popular and accessible, it stocks an impressive range of British designers such as Stella McCartney and Giles Deacon, and international labels including Emporio Armani and DKNY. There is an inviting Food Hall (entrance on Orchard Street), as well as four restaurants and the Moët Bar.

ST CHRISTOPHER'S PLACE & MARYLEBONE HIGH STREET

St Christopher's Place *(map p. 66, B2; Underground: Bond Street)* is a discreet and attractive area to shop and eat near to the Wallace Collection *(see p. 82)*. **Ollie and Nic**, at no. 5 (*Tel: 020 7935 2160*), has an exciting collection of bags, belts and hats. **Petit Chou**, at no. 15 (*Tel: 020 7486 3637*), is the place for charming childrens' clothes and toys. A few steps away is **Marimekko Concept Store**, at no. 16 (*Tel: 020 7486 6454*), which stocks a complete range of lifestyle objects and fashion with bold contemporary designs. At the far end of St Christopher's Place, in Gees Court, is **Paddy Campbell** (*no. 8; Tel: 020 7493 5646*), who sells women's fashions, designed on the premises and beautifully-made in luxury fabrics.

Marylebone High Street (*map p. 66, A2; Underground: Baker Street, Regents Park*) has a distinct neighbourhood atmosphere and a well-balanced selection of shops and restaurants. The Marylebone Farmers' Market in the car park on Cramer Street is a favourite Sunday outing. **Daunt Books**, at no. 83 (*Tel: 020 7224 2295*), specialises in travel books and occupies a handsome Edwardian building with books displayed on oak shelving. **Fishworks**, at no. 89 (*Tel: 020 7935 9796*), is where you can buy fresh fish, eat it at the restaurant and learn how to cook it, all in one day if you prefer. **The Button Queen**, at no. 19 Marylebone Lane (*Tel: 020 7935 1505*), has a myriad of buttons in a multitude of cardboard boxes for you to hunt through.

REGENT STREET AND CARNABY STREET

B **Liberty's** (*208–222 Regent Street, Tel: 020 7734 1234*). A venerable establishment (*pictured right*). This classy department store has galleried floors and its own brand of printed fabrics dating back to the Arts & Crafts movement. It brings together fashion items, exotic imports, and contemporary collectibles.

Carnaby Street (*map p. 66, B4*) swung in and out of the 60s, had a period in the doldrums, but has begun to pick up again and still offers an eclectic browsing opportunity. Two of the best choices for vintage shoes and dresses are **Marshmallow Mountain** (*Tel: 020 7434 9498*) and **Twinkled** (*Tel: 020 7734 2978*) in Kingly Court just off Carnaby Street.

Mock-Tudor frontage of Liberty's, one of London's most elegant department stores

a/s/e London

COVENT GARDEN

Covent Garden Market (*map p. 67, C6*; *Underground: Covent Garden, Leicester Square*) and the nearby streets have a wealth of small shops, cafés, pubs and street entertainment. The old **Market Hall** was, until the 1960s, at the centre of an important wholesale fruit and veg market, next to the Royal Opera House (or 'The Garden'). On two levels and covered by a glass and iron roof, it shelters **Benjamin Pollock** for traditional toys, and **Nauticalia** selling nautical goods and clothing.

C **Jubilee Market** on the South Piazza of Covent Garden, is a general market Tuesday–Friday, which also has antiques on Monday, and arts and crafts at the weekend.

D **Penhaglion's** (*41 Wellington Street, Tel: 020 7836 2150*) has a prestigious range of English scents including Quercus and Bluebell. It was established in 1870, has two royal warrants, and moved to this flagship store in 1975. **E** **Neal's Yard Remedies** (*15 Neal's Yard, Tel: 020 7379 7222*) in a pretty setting, is the original store for natural cosmetics and remedies presented in the distinctive dark blue jars. Around the corner is **Neal's Yard Dairy**, (*17 Shorts Gardens, Tel: 020 7240 5700*) which specialises in regional British cheeses. Very close by, **Office** (*57 Neal Street, Tel: 020 7379 1896*) is a boutique not to be missed for its designer fashions without the designer prices.

WESTMINSTER

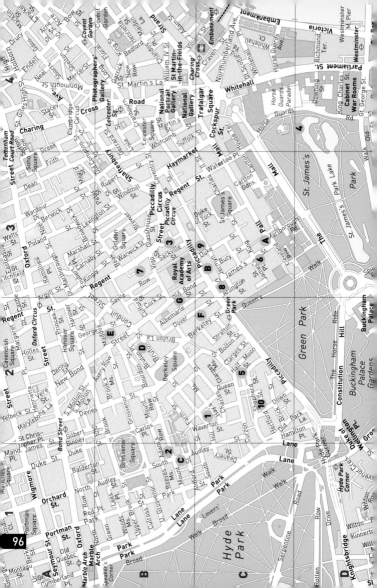

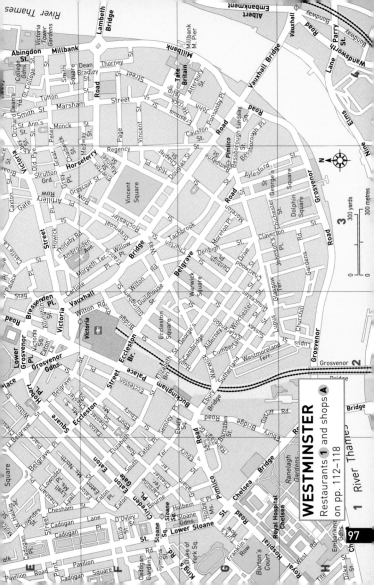

River Thames

Lambeth Bridge

Abingdon St.
Millbank

College St.
Gt. College St.
Victoria Tower Gdns.
Dean Bradley St.
Smith Square
Thorney Street
Dean Stanley St.
Millbank M. Pier
Tate Britain
Millbank
Vauxhall Bridge

Albert Embankment
Bondway
Vauxhall Bondway
Lane
Parry St.
Wandsworth Road

Smith St.
Tufton St.
Orchard St.
Dean's Yd.
Marsham Street
St. Ann's St.
Monck St.
Peter St.
Great Peter St.
Page St.
Regency St.
Causton St.
Ponsonby Pl.
Atterbury St.
John Islip St.
Vincent St.
Erasmus St.
Herrick St.
Ponsonby Pl.
Vauxhall Road

Elms
Nine

Caxton St.
Broadway
St. Chadwick St.
Old Pye St.
Gt. Chapel St.
Strutton Grd.
Horseferry Road
Greycoat St.
Medway St.
Marsham St.
Regency St.
Vincent Square
Hide Pl.
Douglas St.
Gillingham St.
Upper Tachbrook St.
Pimlico
Bessborough Gdns.
Bessborough St.
Lindsay
Drummond Gate
Rampayne St.
Aylesford St.

N

Artillery Row
Gatliff Pl.
Greycoat Pl.
Thirleby Rd.
Ambrosden Ave.
Rochester Row
Howick Pl.
Morpeth Terr.
Willow Pl.
Vincent Square
Rochester St.
Elverton St.
Moreton Pl.
Tachbrook St.
Moreton St.
Charlwood St.
Denbigh St.
St. George's Square
Chichester St.
Dolphin Square
Grosvenor Road

Castle Lane
Buckingham Palace Rd.
Stag Pl.
Vandon St.
Thirleby Rd.
Bressenden Pl.
Allington St.
Castle La.
Vauxhall Bridge Road
Guildhouse St.
Denbigh Pl.
Denbigh Drive
Charlwood St.
Clarendon St.
Johnson's Pl.
Claverton St.
Lupus St.
Glasgow Terr.
Grosvenor Road

300 metres
300 yards
3

Lower Grosvenor Pl.
Victoria Sq.
Grosvenor Gdns.
Buckingham Palace Rd.
Victoria St.
Wilton Rd.
Gillingham St.
Vauxhall Bridge Road
Warwick Square
Warwick Way
Wilton Rd.
Eccleston Square
Belgrave Road
Charlwood St.
St. George's Drive
Cambridge St.
Alderney St.
Winchester St.
Sutherland St.
Cumberland St.
Westmoreland Terr.
Sussex St.
Lupus St.
Churchill Gardens

Grosvenor 2
Grosvenor Road
Chelsea Bridge

WESTMINSTER

Restaurants 1 and shops A
on pp. 112–118

Hobart Pl.
Grosvenor Gdns.
Belgrave Pl.
Eccleston St.
Eaton Square
Chester Sq.
Elizabeth St.
Eccleston St.
Eccleston Bridge
Eccleston Br.
Victoria
Palace Street
Buckingham Palace Road
Elizabeth Bridge
Ebury St.
Ebury Sq.
Warwick Way
Eaton Terr.
Gerald Rd.
Ranelagh Grove
Pimlico Road
Bloomfield Terr.
Sutherland St.
Ranelagh Gardens
Royal Hospital
Chelsea Bridge

1 River Thames

U. Belgrave St.
Belgrave Place
Eaton Pl.
Eaton Square
Eaton Terr.
Gerald Rd.
Elizabeth St.
Chester Row
Eaton Gate
South Eaton Pl.
Graham Terr.
Holbein Pl.
Lower Sloane St.
Royal Hospital Road
Chelsea Bridge

Belgrave Square
West Halkin St.
Lowndes St.
Lyall St.
Chesham St.
Cadogan Lane
Chesham Pl.
Pont St. Ms.
Eaton Ms. North
Lyall Ms.
Cliveden Pl.
Bourne St.
Graham Terr.
Holbein Pl.
Sloane Square
Sloane Gardens
Sloane Ms.
D'Oyley St.
Sloane St.
Franklin's Row
King's Road
Burton's Court
Embankment Gdns.

Mozart St.
W. Halkin St.
Cadogan Lane
Cadogan St.
D'Oyley St.
Symons St.
Blacklands Terr.
Pavilion Road
Pavilion Road
Cadogan Square
King's Road
Royal Avenue
St. Leonard's Terr.
Burton's Ct.
Royal Hospital Road
Duke of York Sq.
Ormonde Gate
West Rd.
Dilke St.
Embankment Gdns.

E
F
G
H

97

introduction

From Mayfair to Westminster is a beautiful part of the city with many royal and aristocratic associations and two leafy oases, Green Park and St James's Park. Next to the royal parks stands Buckingham Palace, the main residence of Queen Elizabeth II and the focal point for many Royal and State occasions. Beyond is Whitehall, named after Henry VIII's palace, now lined with government offices, and Parliament Square dominated by Big Ben, the Houses of Parliament and Westminster Abbey.

The area of St James's takes its name from the older Royal palace, and its tone was in great part determined by the establishment from the late-18th century of 'gentlemen's clubs', which originated in coffee and chocolate houses. By the late-19th century, bespoke tailors moved in to the already fashionable Jermyn Street and Savile Row.

Mayfair, bordered by Park Lane and Regent Street became an exclusive residential area in the 17th and 18th centuries when the Grosvenor, Curzon and Berkeley family estates were developed. It has some of the most famous hotels in London, such as the Dorchester and Claridge's, as well as exclusive shops and restaurants. It was named after the May Fair, which moved to the area in 1686, and by 1735 was laid out as a market for local residents by Edward Shepherd. Shepherd Market has retained a character of its own, with many good restaurants and characterful pubs. Piccadilly, which divides St James's and Mayfair, has unique features such as the Royal Academy, old shopping arcades and the elegant grocery store, Fortnum & Mason.

Buckingham Palace

Open: Daily Aug–Sept 9.45–6, last entry 3.45 (dates may vary);
Changing of the Guard daily May–Aug at 11.30; alternate days the
rest of the year, weather permitting **Charges:** Entry charge, tickets
may be purchased online or from the ticket office at the visitor
entrance, mid-July to mid-Sept, 9.15–5 **Tel:** 020 7766 7300 (bookings only) **Web:** www.royalcollection.org.uk **Underground:** Green
Park, Hyde Park Corner, Victoria **Map:** p. 97, D2
Highlights: Ballroom; Blue Drawing Room; Music Room; Picture
Gallery; sculpture by Antonio Canova; Sèvres porcelain

Buckingham Palace is the Queen's official London residence and a
State guest house with 775 rooms. One of the few working royal
palaces in the world, the Queen spends 26 weeks a year here and when
she takes her annual summer holiday in Balmoral, Scotland, the State
Rooms of the Palace open to the public.

George III purchased Buckingham House in 1762. His son, George IV,
engaged the leading architect of the time, John Nash, to transform it
into a palace and extensive work began in 1825. Queen Victoria was
the first monarch to live here, George V domesticated the palace,
Edward VIII did not care for it, and during George VI's reign the palace
was damaged by bombs.

The grand approach to the Palace along the Mall ends at Queen
Victoria's memorial by Thomas Brock (1911), a complicated affair com-
prising allegorical figures of *Truth*, *Motherhood* and *Justice*. Visitors
watch the daily Changing of the Guard from here.

The tour begins at the Ambassadors' Court leading to the courtyard
overlooked by Nash's magnificent double portico. The Grand Hall, a
relic of the original Buckingham House, was aggrandised by Nash, who
added Corinthian columns of white Carrara marble with gilded bronze
capitals. A dignified staircase with a magnificent balustrade ascends to
a short sequence of lavishly decorated rooms. The Green Drawing
Room displays priceless **Sèvres porcelain**. Two thrones made for the
Queen's Coronation in 1953 dominate the Throne Room, framed by a

London

a/s/e

The magnificent Blue Drawing Room at Buckingham Palace (Photo: Andrew Holt)

proscenium arch supported by two winged victories by Francis Bernasconi. Nash's **Picture Gallery** (47m long) displays truly remarkable paintings, among them an equestrian portrait of Charles I (1633) and *Charles I and Henrietta Maria with their Two Eldest Children* (1632) by van Dyck, *The Music Lesson* (1670) by Vermeer, and *Agatha Bas* (1641) by Rembrandt. The vast **Ballroom** is used for some 20 annual Investitures for achievements in all walks of life, considered by the Queen as one of the most important occasions of her State calendar. The magnificent **Blue Drawing Room** has a coved ceiling, friezes representing the great English poets Shakespeare, Milton and Spenser, and 30 Corinthian columns painted to resemble onyx. The precious Table of the Grand Commanders, inset with **Sèvres porcelain** cameos, was commissioned by Napoleon in 1806 and presented to George IV by Louis XVIII in 1817. The **Music Room**, where guests are presented to the Queen during State visits, is also where the Queen's three eldest children and her grandson, Prince William, were christened. Deep bow windows, a vaulted ceiling, lapis-lazuli *scagliola* columns and the intricate marquetry floor combine to create a beautiful interior. The Ministers' Staircase descends to the Marble Hall with *Mars and Venus* (c. 1815–17) by **Antonio Canova**, and his luxuriant *Fountain Nymph with Putto* (1817–18). The route through the south side of the garden has excellent views of Nash's west façade.

Tate Britain

Open: Daily 10–5.50, first Fri of month 10–10; closed 1 Jan, 24–26 Dec **Charges:** Free entry except special exhibitions **Tel:** 020 7887 8888 **Web:** www.tate.org.uk **Underground:** Pimlico, Vauxhall, Westminster **Boat:** Every 40 mins between Tate Britain and Tate Modern **Map:** p. 96, G4
Highlights: *Flatford Mill* by John Constable; J.M.W. Turner Collection; *Mr and Mrs Clark and Percy* by David Hockney; *Ophelia* by John Everett Millais; *Three Ladies Adorning a Term of Hymen* by Joshua Reynolds; William Blake Collection

Tate Britain, on the Thames at Millbank, contains the national collection of British art from 1500 to the present. Sugar magnate, Henry Tate, presented his personal collection of British art to the nation and funded the building after the National Gallery (*see p. 74*) declined it for lack of space. Established in 1897 as the Tate Gallery, it became known as Tate Britain in 2000 when the Tate Modern (*see p. 27*) opened. Sidney Smith designed the building, to which was added the Clore Gallery, for the Turner collection, in 1987. Tate Britain holds the enjoyably controversial Turner Prize exhibition annually that showcases young British artists. Following are a selection of the highlights of the gallery's collection:

Tudor and Stuart Collection (*rooms 1–3*): One of the earliest paintings, *Queen Elizabeth I* (c. 1575) by Nicholas Hilliard, is more symbolic than lifelike. It shows the queen resplendent, holding the Tudor rose, and is known as the 'Phoenix Portrait' after the mythical bird represented by a jewel on the Queen's bodice. Charming but curious, the double portrait of *The Cholmondeley Ladies* (c. 1600–10), shows two women who were born, married and gave birth on the same day; there are minute differences in the features. Later in the century, portraiture was dominated by Peter Lely, from Haarlem (*Two Ladies of the Lake Family*; c. 1660), and Godfrey Kneller, from Germany (*Portrait of John Banckes*; 1676).

101

a/s/e London

Tate Britain

[A] *Three Ladies Adorning a Term of Hymen* (rm 6)
[B] Blake Collection (rm 8)
[C] *Flatford Mill* (rm 9)
[D] *Ophelia* (rm 15)
[E] *Mr and Mrs Clark* (rm 24)
[F] Turner Collection (rm T1–T9)

[F] [F]

[F]

[F]

Clore Gallery

[F]

27 26 25 21 20

28

[E] 22 19

23 18

Millbank entrance

4 [B] 11 17

[C] **Stairs to restaurant**

[D]

5 [A] 7

Early 18th Century (*room 4*): The Tate owns a comprehensive collection of works by the first major English-born artist William Hogarth, famous for his contemporary scenes and comments on social and political life. *The Scene from the Beggar's Opera* (1728) is the first known painting of a theatrical production, and *O the Roast Beef of Old England* (1748) introduces political satire prompted by the poverty and superstition he met with during his visits to France.
Later 18th Century (*rooms 5–7*): English painting increased in confidence and portrait painters

gained status as public exhibitions were introduced at the Royal Academy (*see p. 110*).

[A] *Three Ladies Adorning a Term of Hymen* (1773) by Joshua Reynolds, takes the 'Irish Graces'—Barbara, Elizabeth and Anne Montgomery—as its models, and is painted in the Old Masters style, depicting the women in graceful poses gathering flowers. *The Artist's Daughter Mary* (1777) reveals Thomas Gainsborough's fluent brushwork, and his mastery of landscape in the portrait of industrialist Benjamin Truman (c. 1770–74). A revived interest in classical subjects inspired Benjamin West to paint his acclaimed *Cleombrotus ordered into Banishment by Leonidas II, King of Sparta* (1768).

[B] Blake Collection (*room 8*): The Tate has a large and internationally renowned collection by the visionary poet-painter William Blake. For his illustrations to the Bible (c. 1799–1805), Blake used a unique colour print technique. His illustrations of Dante's *Divine Comedy* (1824) were commissioned by his friend and artist, John Linnell, and were completed while he was confined to bed with an illness. The large print of *Newton* (1795)

shows how proficient Blake had become with the colour printing process; the delicacy of the portrayal of Newton's hair and skin is extraordinary.

Constable Collection (*rooms 7, 9 & 11*): Suffolk-born John Constable is a quintessentially English landscape artist who made detailed studies of the vagaries of English weather epitomised in his works of skies observed both in the countryside and in London. Best-known paintings include **[C]** *Flatford Mill* (1816–17), a depiction of a major site of his father's corn business in Essex, with barges being towed along the river about to be unhitched.

Victorian Collection (*rooms 9 & 15*): Intensely symbolic and slavishly detailed paintings by leading members of the Pre-Raphaelite Brotherhood include Ford Madox Brown's *The Last of England* (1864–66), Holman Hunt's *The Awakening Conscience* (1853), and Dante Gabriel Rossetti's *Ecce Ancilla Domini* (*The Annunciation*; 1849–50). One of the most popular works in the gallery, inspired by Shakespeare's *Hamlet*, is the tragic watery demise of **[D]** *Ophelia* (1851–52) by John Everett Millais, modelled by

Pre-Raphaelite beauty Elizabeth Siddal in a bath of water. William Frith's *Derby Day* (1856–58) is a satirical portrayal of contemporary life which proved popular when first exhibited. Later Victorian works include Frederic, Lord Leighton's sculpture, *An Athlete Wrestling with a Python* (1877). In contrast, James McNeill Whistler's simplified, lyrical works were criticised as representing nothing but 'art for art's sake'.

The 20th century (*rooms 17–28*): The period up to the First World War produced excitingly innovative art and a number of 'groups' emerged. Camden Town Group members, including Walter Sickert and Charles Ginner, adopted a sombre version of Post-Impressionism, whereas Bloomsbury Group artists Vanessa Bell and Duncan Grant painted richly coloured decorative works. The Vorticists, led by Wyndham Lewis, absorbed the aggressive ideas of Futurism. Hugely talented sculptors of the period were Jacob Epstein and Gaudier-Brzeska. Epstein's alabaster *Jacob and the Angel* (1940–41) is one of the Tate's most popular and important pieces. The excellent collection of abstractionist art from

the 1930s is led by the sculptors Barbara Hepworth and Henry Moore, and painters Ben Nicholson, Paul Nash and Patrick Heron. Hepworth's *Discs in Echelon* (1935), two circles originally carved in wood on a flat base, exhibit her observation of form. Among the collection of paintings by Francis Bacon is *Triptych—August 1972*. A favourite late-twentieth century work is David Hockney's succinctly painted double-portrait, [E] *Mr and Mrs Clark and Percy* (1970–71), of fashion designer Ossie Clark and his wife Celia Birtwell (with their cat) shortly after their wedding.

[F] **Turner Collection** (*rooms T1, T3, T7–T9*): The modern Clore Gallery extension contains an all-embracing collection bringing together works from one of Britain's greatest artists, J.M.W. Turner. The exhibited works encompass all periods and styles of the painter's career as well as displaying personal items such as his paint boxes. Highlights include the dark and violent *The Shipwreck* (1805) and, in contrast, the shimmering *Norham Castle, Sunrise* (c. 1845) which only became popular after Turner's death.

Westminster Abbey

Open: Mon–Tues, Thur–Fri, 9.30–3.3, Wed 9.30–6, Sat 9.30–1.30, Sun and religious hols closed to visitors but open for worship
Charges: Entry charge includes audio guide; verger-led tours available at an extra cost **Tel:** 020 7222 5152 **Web:** www.westminster-abbey.org **Underground:** St James's Park, Westminster
Map: p. 96, E4
Highlights: Grave of the Unknown Warrior; Henry VII Chapel and tomb; Poets' Corner

Westminster Abbey has held the unique role of coronation church since William I came to the throne in 1066, and seventeen English monarchs are buried here. One of the finest Gothic churches in England, it was built over many centuries and shelters a staggering collection of some 2,000 works of art, including superb monumental sculpture spanning nine centuries. Most importantly, it is a working church whose daily life revolves around a regular pattern of worship interspersed with special services. Many important ceremonies have taken place here, including the wedding of the Queen to Prince Philip in 1947 and the Queen's Coronation in 1953. The present church, begun in 1245 by Henry III, replaces two earlier ones. The west towers were not completed until 1745, to Nicholas Hawksmoor's design.

The Interior

As you enter from the north door, you are confronted by the highest Gothic vault in England (31m), especially striking above the empty space of the crossing which is designed for coronation ritual. The modern Waterford crystal chandeliers were presented by the Guinness family for the Abbey's 900th anniversary in 1965.

Altar and Sanctuary: George Gilbert Scott designed the high altar and the reredos (1867) of the sanctuary, in front of which is the precious Cosmati pavement of coloured *tesserae* (1268) from Italy. The shrine of St Edward the Confessor (1269),

a/s/e London

105

Westminster Abbey

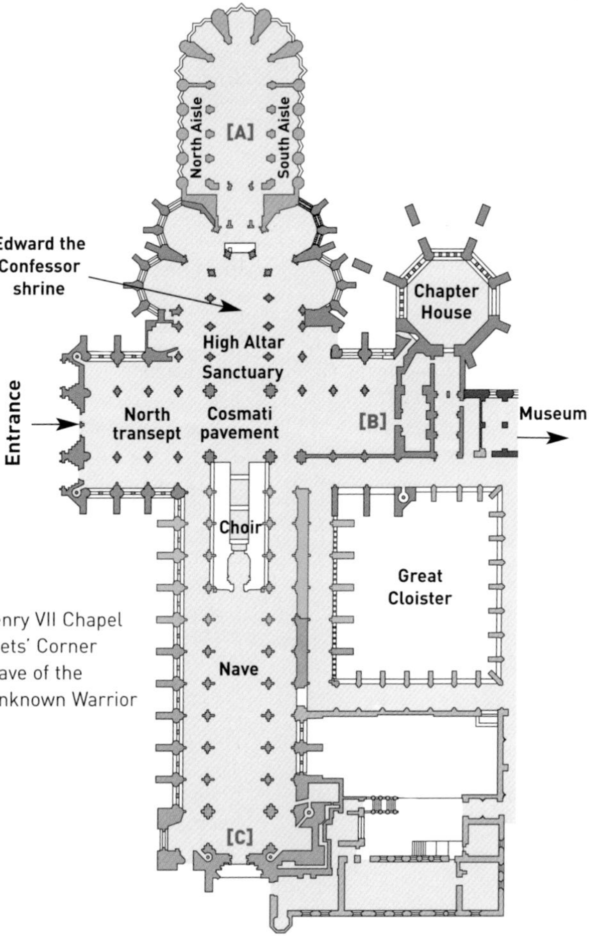

North Aisle

South Aisle

[A]

Edward the
Confessor
shrine

Chapter
House

High Altar

Sanctuary

Entrance

North
transept

Cosmati
pavement

[B]

Museum

Choir

Great
Cloister

[A] Henry VII Chapel
[B] Poets' Corner
[C] Grave of the
Unknown Warrior

Nave

[C]

venerated by pilgrims in the Middle Ages, was damaged at the Reformation and little evidence remains of its original splendour.

North aisle: Off the steps leading to Henry VII's chapel is the monument to Elizabeth I, erected by her successor James I. The superb recumbent effigy in white marble is by Maximilian Colt. Mary I, her Catholic half-sister and rival, is also buried here.

[A] Henry VII Chapel: Bronze gates carrying Tudor emblems open into the glorious Henry VII Chapel, a flamboyant example of late-Gothic perpendicular architecture with delicate fan vaulting, carved pendant bosses and a multitude of saintly sculptures. Heraldic banners of the present Knights of the Order of the Bath add a burst of colour above the rich patina of the oak stalls (c. 1520) which carry anecdotal misericords. The first flowering of Renaissance sculpture in England is the **tomb of Henry VII** (*pictured overleaf*), by the Italian, Pietro Torrigiano, student of Michelangelo, with bronze effigies of the first Tudor king and his queen, Elizabeth of York. James I, Edward VI and George II are also buried in the chapel. At the foot of the steps is the

oak Coronation Chair ordered by Edward I. Used for every coronation since Edward II, it was designed to enclose the Stone of Scone, on which kings of Scotland had been crowned and which Edward I had brought to the Abbey in 1296 after invading Scotland (the Stone was returned to Scotland in 1996).

South Transept: In the south transept, **[B] Poets' Corner** owes its existence to Geoffrey Chaucer, buried here in his role as Court official, not for his writing; his grand tomb is 16th century. Among the many other poets commemorated here are: Edmund Spenser; Alfred, Lord Tennyson; Rudyard Kipling and Thomas Hardy. The 20th-century actor Laurence Olivier is also commemorated here. Outstanding monuments include a memorial to Shakespeare (1740), who is buried in Stratford-upon-Avon, by William Kent, and to George Frederic Handel (1761) by Roubiliac, who was also responsible for the splendid monument to the 2nd Duke of Argyll (1748).

Choir: The Victorian choir, the work of Edward Blore, has an organ dating back to 1727. Against the choir screen is a monument to Isaac Newton.

Nave: From the level of the nave, the sweep of the vaults with gilded bosses is visible. David Livingstone, the missionary and explorer, is buried here. Near the west door is the **[C] Grave of the Unknown Warrior** (1920), repatriated from France; a black Belgian-marble memorial outlined by red Flanders poppies. Outside is the monument to the Innocent Victims of Oppression, Violence and War (1996), and on the west façade are statues (1998) of ten 20th-century Christian martyrs, including Martin Luther King.

The bronze Renaissance tomb of Henry VII and Elizabeth of York, by Pietro Torrigiano

Great Cloister: Off the great cloister is the lavishly decorated octagonal Chapter House built by Henry III c. 1246–55, with one single column supporting the vaults, one of the largest in England. The most ancient part of the abbey, the 11th-century undercroft below the former monks' dormitory, contains the Pyx Chamber, which takes its name from boxes which hold samples of coinage.

Museum: Carefully restored, the 13th-century Westminster Retable, England's oldest altarpiece is thought to have been designed for the Abbey's high altar. It shows images of St Peter, the patron saint of the Abbey, the Miracles of Christ, and full-length figures of Christ, the Virgin Mary and St John the Evangelist. Outside, the Little Cloister leads to the College Garden, the oldest in London.

in the area

Cabinet War Rooms (*King Charles Street, open daily 9.30–6, entry charge including audio guide, Tel: 020 7930 6961, Web: www.iwm.org.uk, Underground: St James's Park, Westminster*). This visit is a remarkable, if slightly claustrophobic, evocation of the Second World War period and of Winston Churchill's presence. The underground shelter was dug out in the 1930s in the basement of the Office of Works. Situated between Parliament and 10 Downing Street, it became operational in August 1939, just before war broke out. By the end of the war it covered over three acres and could accommodate up to 528 people including the War Cabinet and Chiefs of Staff, who worked and slept here during air raids. The sound-proof Cabinet Room, sleeping quarters, hospital and canteen have barely been altered. The rooms were sealed at the end of the war but opened to the public in 1981. The first national museum dedicated to Winston Churchill has been created here with sections covering the whole of his life. The main exhibit is the interactive 15m 'Lifeline' table, with information on Churchill in the context of world events. **Map p. 97, D4**

Green Park & St James's Park (*Underground: Charing Cross, Green Park, Westminster*). **Green Park** supposedly received its name simply because it is. The most natural of the capital's parks, it has no adornments except plane trees, nor any flower beds—although in March daffodils run riot under the trees. It was Charles II who made it a Royal Park, walked among the public and had an ice-house for cooling drinks. The Queen's Walk along the west side was constructed in 1730 for Caroline, George II's queen. Summer days see the park filled with smart striped deckchairs and occupants taking time out from the frantic hustle of Piccadilly and the West End. Adjacent is **St James's Park**, the oldest and one of the prettiest of London's parks, embellished by a lake frequented by ducks and ornamental waterfowl. The park was named after St James's Palace, and became a hunting ground for Henry VIII in 1532, convenient for Whitehall Palace. In the early 17th century James I kept two crocodiles here while Charles II was presented with a pair of pelicans by the Russian ambassador; there have been pelicans in the park ever since. **Map p. 97, D2–D3**

a/s/e London

Houses of Parliament & Big Ben (*tours during summer opening end-July to end-Sept, pre-book by phone or online, or buy from the ticket office in Old Palace Yard. When in session, all visitors may attend debates. UK residents can obtain tickets through their MP for Question Time and free tours throughout the year, Tel: 0870 906 3773, Web: www.parliament.uk, Underground: Westminster*). The stunningly beautiful Houses of Parliament are a 19th-century version of Tudor architecture (*pictured opposite*). The original Palace of Westminster, built by Edward the Confessor, was a royal residence from c. 1065 until 1512 when Henry VIII moved to Whitehall Palace. It evolved as the centre of government from the 12th century. The Houses of Parliament as we see it now was rebuilt by architects Charles Barry and A.W.N. Pugin from 1837. Barry was responsible for the overall design, and Pugin took care of the detail and the meticulous interior decorations. The tour takes you along the route the Queen walks when she opens Parliament each year, through the rich Robing Room and Royal Gallery, to the monarch's throne in the House of Lords, and on to the House of Commons. **Big Ben** (*tours open to UK residents through their local MP, 393 steps, free entry*), with its gilded clock casing and elegant tapered bell stage, has become a potent symbol of London. Big Ben properly refers to the Great Bell of Westminster weighing 13.5 tons with a hammer of 300kg. The clock faces, seven metres in diameter, are by A.W.N. Pugin. The original cast-iron hands were too heavy and were remade, the 2.74m hour hands in gunmetal, and the 4.2m minute hands in hollow copper. **Map p. 96, E4–97, D4**

Royal Academy of Arts (*Burlington House, open daily 10–6, Fri 10–10, Fine Rooms Tues–Fri 1–4.30, Sat–Sun 10–6, entry charge, Tel: 020 7300 8000, Web: www.royalacademy.org.uk, Underground: Green Park, Piccadilly Circus*). The Academy was founded in 1768 under the patronage of George III, with the aim of promoting art and design through its teaching schools. The first President was the English artist, Joshua Reynolds. The annual Summer Exhibition of contemporary British work has been shown since 1769, but less well-known is the Academy's permanent collection. Its greatest treasure, Michelangelo's exquisitely carved marble *Madonna and Child with the Infant St John* (c. 1504–05) known as the *Taddei Tondo*, was bequeathed to the Royal Academy in 1830. Other works include a self-portrait by Reynolds with a bust of Michelangelo, Constable's *Leaping Horse* (1825), sculpture by Flaxman and Chantrey, and architectural drawings by Sir John Soane (*see p. 86*). **Map p. 97, B3**

Big Ben and the Houses of Parliament, designed by Charles Barry and A.W.N. Pugin

eat

Eating opportunities in this area are centred around St James's and Shepherd Market on either side of Piccadilly. St James's is a pleasant eating location, bordered by Green Park and St James's Park, and in the centre of a professional and long-established retail district. Shepherd Market is a haven for traditional pubs, but excellent restaurants, bistros and cafés have also sprung up in the past few years. For price categories, see p. 11; all restaurants are located on map pp. 96 & 97.

1 £££ The Greenhouse, *27a Hay's Mews, Tel: 020 7499 3331, open Mon–Fri 12–2.30 & 6.45–11, Sat 6.45–11, Underground: Green Park.* An exceptionally professional and extravagant restaurant with a 100-page award-winning wine list. Its approach is green, the setting relaxed, and the service attentive. Lyonnais chef, Antonin Bonnet, maintains very high standards with sophisticated and imaginative visual and gustative combinations. There is a variety of menus adapted to the seasons, from a 7-course tasting menu to set-price lunch menus, as well as a 7-course vegetarian menu. Sample from the à la carte: Atlantic yellow-fin tuna *carpaccio* with crispy pears and black olives, and a superb French cheese trolley.

2 £££ Scotts, *20 Mount Street, Tel: 020 7495 7309, open Mon–Sat 12–10.30, Sun 12–10, Underground: Bond Street, Green Park.* ◼ What

began as an oyster warehouse in 1851 evolved into an oyster bar and seafood restaurant at this address in 1968. It has received a makeover from designer Martin Brudniski, inspired by its 'ostentatious past', with oak-panelling and burgundy leather banquettes contrasting with the avant-garde British artworks on display. In the relaxed Oyster Bar you can enjoy the full à la carte menu all day, as well as a seasonal range of oysters and there is an awe-inspiring 3m-long display of sea-food. You might go for potted shrimps and dressed crab, but there is a good choice of modern more meaty dishes, such as Herdwick mutton & turnip pie. Vegetarians and vegans are well catered for. There is a good selection of wines by the glass.

3 ££ Bentley's Oyster Bar & Grill, *11–15 Swallow Street, Tel: 020 7734 4756, open Mon–Sat 12–12, Sun 12–10, Underground: Piccadilly*

Circus. Irishman Richard Corrigan's belief in fresh products, honest flavours, quality ingredients and uncluttered cooking brought him great acclaim before taking over Bentley's in 2005. He has breathed new life into this famous name, and the refurbished Grill and Rib Rooms upstairs are kitted out in William Morris wallpapers and wood floors, in keeping with the old, while the Crustacea Room is cosy in tones of red. Classic winners include Dover sole *meunière* and Bentley's fish pie. More elaborate is the Baked brill with Jabugo ham, pea and marjoram broth.

④ ££ Inn the Park, *St James's Park, Tel: 020 7451 9999, open daily 8–11, 12–3 & 5–10.30, Underground: St James's Park*. ■ A lovely spot to lunch next to St James's Park lake, the stunning modern teardrop-shaped building blends in with the park, and includes a turfed roof and large windows and a terrace for alfresco eating. Popular with Whitehall civil servants and office workers, it's important to book. The fresh, uncomplicated British cooking is excellent—this is no sandwich bar: for example, Smoked eel and bacon salad with a poached egg for starters, and Beef with hand-cut chips, for main.

⑤ ££ Kiku, *17 Half Moon Street, Tel: 020 7499 4208, open Mon–Sat 12–2.30 & 6–10.15, Sun & hols 5.35–9.45, Underground: Green Park*. Kiku's reputation for authentic Japanese food, since it was established in 1978, has remained first rate and it keeps up-to-date with trends and décor. There is a sushi bar for the initiated, or simply for starters, and a comprehensive main menu with an emphasis on seafood. Choices include Marinated mackerel salad, and Grilled eel on rice with miso soup.

⑥ ££ Luciano, *72–73 St James's Street, Tel: 020 7408 1440, open Mon–Sat 12–3, 6–11, Underground: Green Park*. In elegant, clubby St James's, this glamorous restaurant is the brainchild of Marco Pierre White and Rocco Forte. Dedicated to Italian authenticity it opened in 2005 in the sexily revamped former Prunier premises with black columns, subdued colours, leather upholstery and sexy prints. The chic and shiny Johnny Walker bar is open between times. The generous servings in the restaurant include antipasti or Parma ham with figs, and other Italian classics such as Oxtail fettuccine, *osso buco ragu*, and Veal cutlets with butter and sage. The menu changes every three months and the service and attention to detail is top-class.

⑦ ££ Momo, *25 Heddon Street, Tel: 020 7434 4040, restaurant open Mon–Sat 12pm–1am, Sun 12–12; tea room open Mon–Sat 12–11, Underground: Piccadilly Circus*. This luxuriously adorned restaurant serves authentic North African food. Choices include subtly spiced tagines, couscous, or traditional pigeon *pastilla* wrapped in filo

London

a/s/e

Sleek interior decoration at The Wolseley restaurant on Piccadilly

pastry with almonds, cinnamon and orange confit. Mint tea and sweetmeats are served in the exotic bazaar or on the terrace. The bar serves *kemia* (Arabic tapas) to a backdrop of live music from 8pm.

££ Tate Britain, *Millbank, (map p. 96, G4)*, *Tel: 020 7887 8825, open Mon–Fri 11.30–3 & 3.30–5; Sat & Sun 10–3 & 3.30–5, Underground: Pimlico*. ■ With Rex Whistler décor, this is a peaceful haven opposite the Tate cafeteria, attracting both local business people as well as gallery enthusiasts. The British sourced food is well cooked and presented, and includes Devilled kidneys or Confit duck terrine with plum chutney, followed by Grilled plaice from Newlyn or Devonshire beef. The wine list is outstanding, with a huge choice constantly updated and a good range of half bottles.

8 ££ The Wolseley, *160 Piccadilly, Tel: 020 7499 6996, open Mon–Fri 7am–midnight, Sat 8am–midnight, Sun 8am–11pm, Underground: Green Park, Piccadilly Circus*. It is imperative to book well in advance for this hugely popular restaurant in the former Wolseley car showroom. Eating here is a fashionable event. The sleek surroundings emulate a Viennese café, and the service is smooth. The food tends towards old-fashioned with mid-European influences, such as Steak tartare, chopped liver, and Wiener Holstein; alternatively, there is traditional Dover sole. The small café and bar, for drinks or tea (excellent cakes) are good alternatives to the hectic lunch and dinnertime. The owners, Christopher Corbin and Jeremy King, also run the St Alban at 4–12 Regent Street.

9 £-££ Fortnum & Mason, *181 Piccadilly, Tel: 0845 602 5694, Underground: Green Park, Piccadilly Circus*. Fortnum & Mason, the upmarket grocery store (*see also p. 117 below*), has several eating places. The swish new 1707 wine bar (*open Mon–Sat 12–11, Sun 12–5.30*), is named after Fortnum's foundation year. It proposes 'flights' of 3 wines to accompany a selection from the bar menu, or a bottle from the Wine department. At the brasserie-style Fountain Restaurant (*open Mon–Sat 7.30–11, 12–3, 5–11, Sun 12–5.30*) ▬ overlooking Jermyn Street, you can sample Fortnum's famous Welsh Rarebit. The Gallery Restaurant, (*open Mon–Sat 10–6, Sun 12–5.30*) looks out onto the Food Hall from which it takes its inspiration. On the fourth floor, the St James's (*open Mon–Sat 12–7, Sun 2–5*) is an elegant and comfortable setting for lunch or a peaceful afternoon tea.

The first floor Parlour (*open Mon–Sat 10–7, Sun 12–5.30*) is the place for heavenly hot chocolate, desserts or an over-the-top knickerbocker-glory sundae.

10 **£ Shepherd's Tavern**, *50 Hertford Street, Tel: 020 7499 3017, open Mon–Sat 11–11, Sun 12–10, Underground: Green Park*. On the edge of Shepherd Market, laid out by architect Edward Shepherd in the early eighteenth century, Shepherd's Tavern (*pictured below*) is a good place to stop for a pint of London Pride ale in handsome Georgian surroundings.

The elegant Georgian townhouse that is home to the Shepherd's Tavern, one of the traditional pubs in the Shepherd Market area of central London

shop

The shops around Mayfair and St James's tend to be elegant, exclusive and wonderful to gaze at. Many have Royal Warrants and some of the oldest retailers in London still operate in St James's, but little can compare to the charm of the shopping arcades off Piccadilly. Jermyn Street and Savile Row are traditionally associated with bespoke gentlemen's tailors, and around Christie's and Sotheby's art auction houses on King Street (*map p. 97, C3*) and New Bond Street (*map p. 97, A2–B2*), there are many commercial galleries. Bond Street (both Old and New) is also the most intense designer shopping experience in London. All shops are located on map pp. 96 & 97.

PICCADILLY & ST JAMES'S

A Berry Bros and Rudd, *3 St James's Street, Tel: 020 7900 4300, open Mon–Fri 10–6, Sat 10–5, Underground: Green Park*. Since 1698, this specialist wine merchant has occupied the same premises on St James's Street and has a rare example of an 18th-century London shop front. In the beautiful panelled interior all manner of advice concerning wine can be sought, but the bottles are out of sight in the vast cellars below. However, the new shop at no. 2 has wines on display in all price ranges. There is also a Spirits Room.

B Burlington Arcade, *Piccadilly, open Mon–Fri 9.30–5.30, Sat 10–6, Underground: Green Park, Piccadilly Circus*. Of the shopping arcades on Piccadilly, Burlington Arcade is the longest (200m), oldest and most beautiful (*pictured opposite*). It was

built in 1819 by George Cavendish, owner of Burlington House (now home to the Royal Academy; *see p. 110*). The whole arcade is a protected historic monument, and has recently undergone a costly renovation to restore its original décor. The arcade is characterfully patrolled by beadles wearing Edwardian frock coats and gold-braided top hats, who maintain decorum—no running, no singing, no whistling—although in 1964 there was a spectacular robbery using a Mark-10 Jaguar as the getaway car: bollards have now put paid to this sort of behaviour. Among the 47 shops is the first ever purveyor of food in the arcade, **Ladurée** (*Tel: 020 7491 9155*), a Parisian macaroon specialist, installed in a tiny 'golden grotto'. Opposite is, **Vilbrequin** (*Tel: 020 7499 6558*), selling chic beachwear and boxer shorts for men. The 'shoe queen' **Beatrix Ong** (*Tel: 020 7499 4089*) opened here recently. There are cashmere specialists, including **Berk** (*Tel: 020 7493 0028*), beautiful leather accessories at **Franchetti Bond** (*Tel: 020 7629 0025*), and everything for the Polo-player at **Polistas** (*Tel: 020 7495 6603*). Among jewellers are **Richard Ogden** (*Tel: 020 7493 9136*), who has created an intimate 'wedding-ring room'.

9 Fortnum & Mason, *181 Piccadilly, Tel: 020 7734 8040, open Mon–Sat 10–8, Sun 12–6, Underground: Green Park.* Fortnum & Mason is a rare experience in London's fast-moving commercial market place, with tail-coated assistants and a sensual Food Hall selling everything from hand-made chocolates to pork pies. Established in 1707, Fortnum's own-label teas and Christmas hampers are recognised worldwide. The pale green shop-front has a chiming clock and some of the most imaginative window displays in London. In addition,

Burlington Arcade: the longest and oldest shopping arcade in London

on the upper floors are home, fashion accessory and beauty departments. It has several restaurants (*see p. 114 above*).

JERMYN STREET

Jermyn Street (*Underground: Green Park, Piccadilly Circus; map p. 97, C3–B3*) is the leading street, along with Savile Row, of bespoke tailors in London. However, it also has an excellent range of independent shops selling other high-end goods. **Bates**, at no. 21a, (*Tel: 020 7734 2722, open Mon–Fri 9–5, Sat 9.30–1 & 2–4*) has a splendidly rustic interior containing all types of gentlemen's hats: trilbies; tweed caps; deer-stalkers. **Floris**, at no. 89 (*Tel: 020 7930 2885, open Mon–Fri 9.30–6, Sat 10–6*), is best known for its traditional scents and soaps. The interior has original 1851 Spanish mahogany fittings and an endearing mahogany and velvet change pad. **Nigel Milne**, at no. 38 (*Tel: 020 7434 9343, open Mon–Fri 10–6, Sat 10–4*), is a high-quality independent jewellers, and the only stockist of the Pomellato range of unique Italian pieces using coloured stones. **Paxton & Whitfield**, at no. 93 *(Tel: 020 7930 0259, open Mon–Fri 9–5)*, stocks the perfect Stilton to accompany a glass of Berry Brothers' port *(see p. 116 above)* .

BOND STREET AND MAYFAIR

C **James Purdey & Sons**, *57–58 South Audley Street, Tel: 020 7499 1801, open Mon–Fri, 9.30–5.30, Sat 10–5, Underground: Green Park, Hyde Park Corner*. The magnificent Royal coat of arms above the entrance and the quintessentially 'English' décor of dark oak and leather is the setting for this specialist supplier of hunting equipment and accessories. The company has made and sold shotguns and rifles since 1814 and their goods have been sold at this address since 1882.

D **Stella McCartney**, *30 Bruton Street, Tel: 020 7518 3100, open Mon–Wed, Fri & Sat 10–6, Thur 10–7, Underground: Bond Street, Green Park*. Stella McCartney's London flagship sells ready-to-wear designs launched as a joint venture with Gucci in 2001. The wearable and feminine clothes range from perfectly tailored suits to floaty chiffon dresses, as well as lingerie, and a skin care and performance range in association with Adidas. A committed vegetarian, McCartney does not use leather for the bags or shoes.

E **Smythson of Bond Street**, *40 New Bond Street, Tel: 020 7629 8558, open Mon–Wed & Fri 9.30–6, Thur 10–7, Sat 10–6, Underground: Bond Street, Oxford Circus*. In addition to leather goods including the 'travel clutch', Smythson has stylish notebooks and diaries, as well as personalised writing-paper, in this well-heeled shop.

F **Dover Street Market**, *17–18 Dover Street, Tel: 020 7518 0680, open Mon–Wed, Fri & Sat 11–6, Thur 11–7, Underground: Green Park*. This designer space was founded in 2004 by Comme des Garçons. On the catwalk are wild and wacky creations as well as established and new designers such as Junya Watanabe's draped and wrapped African Roots, Marios Schwab's 'Body Conscious' collection, Sara Lanzi's pretty pleats and knits, and Gareth Pugh and Rei Kawakubu.

G **Royal Arcade**, *Bond Street, open Mon–Sat 10–6, Underground Green Park*. Off Old Bond Street is a neo-gothic arcade with distinctive peach-coloured mouldings. Here, you will find **Angela Hale** *(Tel: 020 7495 1920)*, a feminine boutique strewn with pretty things including costume jewellery and fabrics, and **Charbonnel et Walker** *(Tel: 020 7491 0939)*, for beautifully-packaged hand-made chocolates and the most luxurious drinking chocolate and truffle sauce.

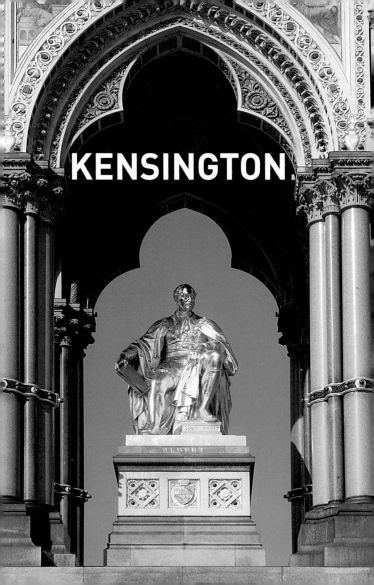

KENSINGTON.

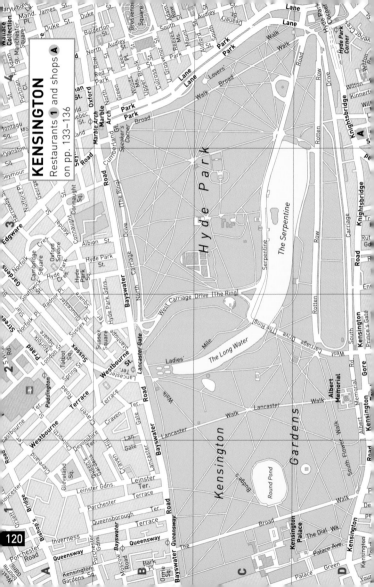

introduction

At the heart of Kensington is one of the world's favourite museums, the Victoria & Albert. Alongside it are the family-friendly Science and Natural History Museums, and opposite Kensington Gardens is the Royal Albert Hall. The idea of a cultural centre for London was championed by Queen Victoria's husband Prince Albert and land was purchased in South Kensington with profits from the Great Exhibition held in Hyde Park in 1851. Appropriately, the elaborate memorial to Prince Albert stands opposite the Albert Hall.

Both South Kensington and Knightsbridge were the result of the expansion of London westwards in the 19th century. Many of the elegant residential streets, tall red-brick terraces, and neo-Gothic public buildings of that period have survived. Knightsbridge is a classy commercial centre; the most famous department store of all times, Harrods, is a major attraction to shopaholics.

Chelsea, which stretches down to the river Thames, became fashionable in the 16th century when Henry VIII and Thomas More, among others, built country houses here. These have disappeared, but the Royal Hospital and Chelsea Physic Garden are remnants of its earlier life. Predominantly residential, like Knightsbridge and South Kensington, Chelsea has delightful side streets with pretty terraced houses, and retains something of a village atmosphere. The King's Road, a good place to stroll, window shop and people watch, attracted bohemians in the early 20th century, was swinging in the 1960s, and in the 1970s saw the birth of punk when Vivienne Westwood opened her boutique Sex, at number 430. It is still magnetic, attracting artists, celebrities and visitors alike to its variety of boutiques and excellent restaurants.

Victoria & Albert Museum

Open: Daily 10–5.45, Weds & last Fri of month 10–10, closed 24–26 Dec **Charges:** Free entry, except special exhibitions
Entrances: Cromwell Road, Exhibition Road (Level 1), and Tunnel Entrance direct from South Kensington Underground (Level 0)
Tel: 020 7942 2000 **Web:** www.vam.ac.uk **Underground:** South Kensington **Map:** p. 121, E2
Highlights: 19th-century café rooms; *The Ascension with Christ Giving the Keys to St Peter* by Donatello; *Bashaw* by Matthew Cotes Wyatt; *Burghley Nef* from France; the Great Bed of Ware from Herefordshire; *Neptune and Triton* by Gian Lorenzo Bernini; the Raphael Cartoons; *Tippoo's Musical Tiger* from India; *Young Man among Roses* by Nicholas Hilliard

This world-famous museum of applied arts has an outstandingly varied collection spanning many centuries, initiated by Queen Victoria who laid the foundation stone in 1899. The museum covers a 12-acre site, and is a masterpiece in itself, using cast and wrought iron, acres of glass, and extensive applied decoration including ceramic mosaics and majolica. The collection is divided between two gallery types: the Materials and Techniques Galleries (e.g. Sculpture, Silver), and the Period Galleries (e.g. Asia, British), although works of different materials and techniques are also exhibited throughout the period galleries. An ambitious refurbishment is on-going, and some galleries are closed until 2009; check on-line for latest details. The V&A collection is vast and is difficult to embrace fully in one visit. Following is a selection of the highlights on display:

Materials & Techniques Galleries

Sculpture (*Level 1, rooms 21–24 & Level 3, room 111*): The post-classical collection includes masterpieces from small ivory carvings to large monuments. The Italian Renaissance is very well-represented and contains Donatello's marble relief **[A]** *The Ascension with Christ Giving the Keys to St Peter* (c. 1428–30) in

a/s/e London

123

Victoria & Albert Museum
Levels 0 and 1

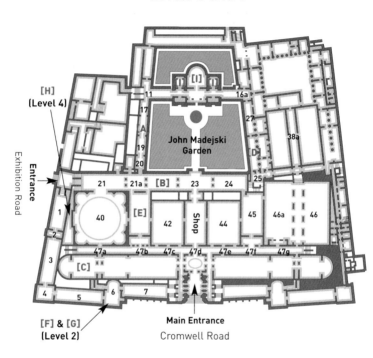

[A] *The Ascension with Christ Giving the Keys to St Peter* (rm 18)

[B] *Neptune and Triton* (rm 22)

[C] Raphael Cartoons (rm 48a)

[D] *Burghley Nef* (rm 26)

[E] *Tippoo's Musical Tiger* (rm 41)

[F] *Young Man Among Roses* (rm 57a)

[G] Great Bed of Ware (rm 57)

[H] *Bashaw* (rm 118a)

[I] 19th-century café rooms

room 18. Carved in *rilievo schiacciato*, literally 'squashed relief', this is one of the best surviving examples of the technique (which Donatello himself developed), giving a very subtle effect of perspective to the work. Also outstanding in this collection is the Baroque marble by Bernini, **[B]** *Neptune and Triton* (c. 1620–22) in room 22, a powerful composition depicting the struggle between the God of the Seas and his merman son, Triton. Originally sculpted as part of a fountain, it is the only large-scale work by Bernini shown outside Italy.

Cast Courts (*Level 1, room 46a*): This vast space exhibits plaster-cast reproductions and electrotypes of the most famous examples of sculpture in the world such as the two-part cast of Trajan's Column, in the Forum of Trajan in Rome.

Fashion (*Level 1, room 40*): Representative items from the dress collection span all periods and all types of clothing, from a mid-eighteenth century woman's riding jacket to Vivienne Westwood's blue 'mock-croc' platform shoes (1993–94).

Photography (*Level 1, room 38a*): The V&A's photography collection is large and holds important works, such as a portfolio of over 250 photos by Julia Margaret Cameron, and those of Benjamin Brecknell Turner, one of Britain's earliest and greatest photographers. Annual exhibitions are selected from the 500,000 images in the collection, dating back to 1852.

Paintings (*Level 3, rooms 81, 82, 87–88a & 90a*): Celebrated works by English masters J.M.W. Turner and John Constable are displayed, including many of Constable's oil sketches and watercolours. The Portrait Miniatures collection in room 90a is fascinating, with some of the earliest miniatures from the 1520s painted by Lucas Horenbout and Jean Clouet, as well as examples by Hans Holbein the Younger, portrait painter to Henry VIII.

Silver (*Level 3, rooms 65–70a*): These gleaming galleries display the *Ashburnham Centrepiece* (1747) by Nicolas Sprimont, a major example of English rococo silverware, and unique contemporary pieces such as *Pair of Candlesticks* (1999) by Jan van Nouhuys. Three wonderful life-size lions (1885) are electrotype copies of those made for Rosenborg Castle, Copenhagen, in the 17th century.

a/s/e London

Ironwork and Metalware (*Level 3, rooms 113–114e & 116*): These rooms contain an impressive display of functional objects such as tools, shop signs and wrought-iron gates, as well as the *Hereford Screen* (1862) by George Gilbert Scott, from Hereford Cathedral, which has been painstakingly returned to its original state.

Textiles (*Level 3, rooms 98–100*): The collection covers a period of more than 2,000 years and includes the largest lace collection in the world. The Tapestry Gallery (room 94) contains four *Devonshire Hunting Tapestries* (c. 1425–30), showing important depictions of one of the Tudor's favourite past-times. The tapestries hung for centuries at Hardwick Hall, Derbyshire, where they had been cut up, layered and nailed to a wall to keep out the cold. They took ten years to restore.

Glass Collection (*Level 4, rooms 129 & 131*): Some 6,000 pieces from the Middle East, Europe and America, from the 2nd millennium BC to the present comprise this collection. Included is *The Luck of Edenhall*, an exceptionally fine 13th-century Syrian beaker with a flaring rim decorated in gold and enamels. The more modest *Frost-Fair Mug* has miraculously survived as a souvenir of the unique fair held on the frozen Thames in 1683–84.

Ceramics (*Level 6, rooms 133a–145; closed until Sept 2009*): This unrivalled international collection encompasses the entire history of ceramics from the 3rd millennium BC to the present day. Historically intriguing is a tile-panel (1876) by William Morris and William de Morgan, one of only six that remain from an unusually large decorating commission for Membland Hall in Plymouth.

Period Galleries

Europe 1500–1800 (*Level 0, rooms 1–7 & Level 1, room 48a*): Splendid examples of musical instruments are shown, including a lavish spinet (harpsichord; 1571) by Annibale Rossi, decorated with nearly 2,000 precious stones. The celebrated **[C] Raphael Cartoons** (1515–16) are magnificently displayed in room 48a. Seven tapestry designs, painted for Pope Leo X (the tapestries were intended to line the Sistine Chapel in Rome), depict the acts of Sts Peter and Paul, the founders of the Christian Church. An important example of High Renaissance art, they were purchased by Charles I in 1623 who had tapestries woven from them at the newly established tapestry factory at Mortlake, Surrey. Raphael's Cartoons are perhaps more famous than any of the tapestries produced from their designs.

Medieval and Renaissance collections, c. 300–1600 (*ten new galleries will open in Nov 2009; key items are temporarily on display on Level 1, rooms 11, 16a, 17–20, 25–27 & 46*): Among precious objects is the ivory *Symmachi Panel* (c. 400 AD), one leaf of a diptych made for two aristocratic Roman families, Symmachi and Nicomachi. The *Nicomachi* leaf is in the Musée du Moyen Age in Paris. The panel shows a priestess sprinkling holy water before an altar, highlighting the pagan rituals still taking place at a time when Christianity was becoming the dominant religion of Rome. In the northern renaissance collection, the **[D]** *Burghley Nef* (1527) in room 26 is a particularly fine parcel-gilt silver salt cellar in the form of a ship. Antonio Rossellino's *Virgin with the Laughing Child* (c. 1465) is an admired terracotta statuette.

Asia (*Level 1, rooms 41–47g*): The best examples of Southeast Asian, Indian, Japanese, Chinese and Korean art are displayed here. A favourite piece from Mughal India (room 41) is **[E]** *Tippoo's Musical Tiger* (c. 1790), a wooden organ in the form of a tiger mauling a British officer, made for Tipu Sultan, ruler of Mysore. Among exquisite objects belonging to the Mughal emperor Shah Jahan is his white jade wine cup (1657). The Ardabil carpet (1539–40) is one of the finest (and considered the largest) Persian carpets in the world. The Chinese burial sculpture of the head and partial torso of a horse (206 BC–AD 220) is the largest jade animal carving known. The Japanese collection includes lacquerware from the 19th century, more than 20,000 woodblock prints, and an exquisite display of kimono.

British Galleries (*Level 2, rooms 52–58 & Level 4, rooms 118–125*): These galleries contain prized examples of British decorative items from the Court of Henry VIII to the death of Queen Victoria. Outstanding from the period 1500–1760, is Nicholas Hilliard's miniature

[F] *Young Man among Roses*. Hilliard was the founder of the British School of miniature painting, and Master Painter to Elizabeth I. The young man in this miniature has come to epitomise the Elizabethan hero, with his dark, curly hair, swooning stance and hand placed on his heart. Also prized is the Heneage 'Armada' Jewel (c. 1600), a gold and enamel medallic image in profile set with diamonds and rubies. The magnificent **[G]** *Great Bed of Ware*, twice the size of any of the period, was mentioned in Shakespeare's *Twelfth Night*. It is thought to have been made in London; the inlay is a specialism of German woodworkers who settled in Southwark on the south bank of the river Thames. Also remarkable is James II's wedding suit (1673), heavily embroidered with silver and silver-gilt thread. The period 1760–1900 contains a section devoted to the great English furniture designer Thomas Chippendale. The Gothic Revival is illustrated by a candelabrum made for the House of Lords by A.W.N. Pugin (*see p. 110*). Unmissable is the sculpture of **[H]** *Bashaw* (1832–34; *pictured right*), a favourite dog of Lord Dudley, shown trampeling on a snake. No expense was spared in the execution of Bashaw with Persian topaz chosen for his eyes and marble for his body, however, the statue is not to everyone's taste—John Ruskin loathed it and considered it a 'worm-cast of a production'.

Europe and America 1800–1900 (*Level 3, room 101*): Many objects here were acquired from the great International Exhibitions such as a massive Gothic Revival bookcase (1851). French Art Nouveau objects include a Bugatti armchair.

Twentieth century (*Level 3, rooms 70–74*): Interesting here are examples from the Omega Workshops founded in 1913 by Roger Fry and Vanessa Bell.

The V&A was one of the first museums to have refreshments on sale, as a result of the pioneering ideas of its first director, Henry Cole. The café ■ at the V&A incorporates three remarkable **[I]** 19th-century rooms: the Gamble Room; the Morris Room decorated by William Morris's firm and Edward Burne-Jones; and the Poynter Room. These can be reached through the more uniform modern café section.

Lord Dudley's favourite dog, Bashaw, immortalised at the V&A musuem

in the area

Albert Memorial (*Underground: High Street Kensington, Knightsbridge*). Situated on the edge of Kensington Gardens and opposite the Royal Albert Hall (*see opposite*), the Albert Memorial is a high-Victorian neo-Gothic affair, designed by George Gilbert Scott and remarkable for its colour and glitter. It was erected in memory of Queen Victoria's husband, Prince Albert, who was instrumental in turning Kensington into a cultural district. The memorial was opened to the public in 1872. A high stepped plinth holds seven tiers of statuary, including ethnographic figures and representative animals: an elephant (Asia); a camel (Africa); a buffalo (the Americas); and a bull (Europe). The white marble *Frieze of Parnassus* around the base of the monument carries no less than 169 figures of painters, architects, musicians, poets and sculptors. Columns of granite with Portland stone support the elaborate glass mosaics by the Salviati family. On the spire are gilt-bronze figures of *Faith*, *Hope*, *Charity* and *Humility*, with *Fortitude*, *Prudence*, *Justice* and *Temperance*, topped by eight gilt bronze angels. The monument was completely restored to its former glory in the 1990s. **Map p. 120, D2**

Chelsea Physic Garden (*open March–Oct Mon, Wed & Thur 12–5, Sun 12–6, entry charge, Tel: 020 7352 5646, Web: www.chelseaphysicgarden.co.uk, Underground: Sloane Square*). A hidden oasis in the centre of London, Chelsea Physic Garden was founded by the Worshipful Society of Apothecaries in 1673 to train students in the cultivation and study of medicinal plants, a mission which continues to this day: the Botany Department of the Natural History Museum use the garden and its specimins for research. The beds contain a fascinating wealth of plants, both native and from around the world collected by William Hudson and Joseph Banks, among others. The rock garden, constructed from Icelandic lava, flint and stones from the Tower of London, is the oldest public rock garden in England. **Map p. 121, H3**

Hyde Park (*open daily 5am–midnight, Web: www.royalparks.org, Underground: Hyde Park Corner, Knightsbridge, Lancaster Gate, Marble Arch*). The largest of London's parks, Hyde Park covers 350 acres.

Originally roamed by wild boar and deer, in the 16th century it became a hunting ground for Henry VIII. Nowadays, you can join Londoners in jogging, cycling, rollerblading and horse-riding, or simply laying under one of its 4,000 trees or watching the birds and the boaters on the Serpentine lake. In the adjoining Kensington Gardens is the Serpentine art gallery, the famous monument to J.M. Barrie's *Peter Pan* (1912) and the Diana, Princess of Wales memorial fountain. **Map p. 120, B2–D4**

Natural History Museum (*open daily 10–5.50, closed 24–26 Dec, free entry, Tel: 020 7942 5000, Web: www.nhm.ac.uk, Underground: South Kensington*). The world famous Natural History Museum, opened in 1881, occupies Alfred Waterhouse's spectacular neo-Romanesque temple, decorated inside and out with cast terracotta replicas of birds and beasts. It contains over 70 million natural history specimens among which are samples from Captain Cook's voyages of discovery and Darwin's exploration of the Galapagos Islands. In the dramatic entrance hall stands the famous cast of the *Diplodocus carnegii*, one of the largest ever land mammals, presented by the Carnegie Museum, Pittsburgh, in 1905. The largest living mammal to be represented in the life galleries is the huge model of a blue whale suspended from the roof; among the smallest is the pigmy shrew. The historical bird collection is an early museum display and includes the extinct dodo. Minerals housed in original Victorian wooden cabinets display examples of raw, cut and polished gemstones. **Map p. 121, E2**

Royal Albert Hall (*guided tours Thur–Tues 10.30–3.30, pre-booked tickets from the box office, Tel: 020 7838 3105, Web: www.royalalberthall.com, Underground: South Kensington*). The Albert Hall is one of the most distinctive and best loved concert halls in London, hosting events as varied as great choral concerts, tennis championships and university degree ceremonies, and, since 1941, the hugely popular 'Proms' (Henry Wood Promenade Concerts). In 1963 the Beatles and the Rolling Stones made their one-and-only appearance on the same bill. The concert hall project was part of Prince Albert's cultural scheme for Kensington but did not get underway until after his death in 1861. In 1867 Queen Victoria laid the foundation stone (in block K at the rear of the stalls). The building is like no other in the city, elliptical in shape and decorated externally in terracotta, with a high frieze around the glass and steel dome. Inside is a tiered amphitheatre decked out in red velvet around an arena above which the dome rises to 41m. The 150-ton organ has 9,997 pipes and originally needed a steam engine to work the bellows. It was played by Bruckner at the inaugural concert. **Map p. 120, D2**

Sir Christopher Wren's elegant Royal Hospital Chelsea (1692)

Royal Hospital Chelsea (*museum and shop open daily 10–12 & 2–4, closed Sun Oct–March, free entry, guided tours at extra charge, Tel: 020 7881 5303, Web: www.chelsea-pensioners.co.uk, Underground: Sloane Square*). Home to over 400 scarlet-jacketed Chelsea Pensioners, the hospital was founded by Charles II in 1682 to care for invalided or aged soldiers. The imposing building with its elegant central Doric portico is a Wren masterpiece. The annual Chelsea Flower Show, which draws visitors from across the world, is held every May in the gardens. **Map p. 121, G4**

Science Museum (*open daily 10–6, closed 24–26 Dec, free entry, Tel: 0870 870 4868, Web: www.sciencemuseum.org.uk, Underground: South Kensington*). Next door to the Natural History Museum (*see p. 131 above*), the Science Museum is another ultimate family day out. It is home to over 20,000 original objects, and is London's most hands-on museum with 800 interactive displays. The collections comprise a display of early steam engines, Stephenson's Rocket locomotive, and a replica of the Huyguns lander which reached Saturn's moon, Titan, in 2005. The Flight Gallery follows the evolution of aviation and contains Amy Johnson's Gipsy Moth, and a deconstructed Spitfire. There is also a spectacular IMAX 3D cinema for all kinds of out-of-this-world experiences. **Map p. 121, E2**

eat

Chelsea is the haunt of one of the current figureheads of British food, Gordon Ramsey. Expect to have to book in advance for many of the top restaurants here. However, Fulham Road and Sloane Square offer plenty of places to eat on the run, and the V&A museum, with its 19th-century café rooms, offers the very best surroundings in which to take lunch or tea. For price categories, see p. 11; all restaurants are located on map pp. 120 & 121.

1 ££££ Restaurant Gordon Ramsay, *68–69 Royal Hospital Road, Tel: 020 7352 4441 (booking essential), open Mon–Fri 12–2 & 6.30–11, Underground: Sloane Square.* ■ Ramsay's empire stretches far and wide, but for one of those really special occasions a meal at his Michelin 3-star flagship restaurant is a truly gastronomic experience. The service is impeccable, the insistence on absolutely fresh top-quality ingredients is the hallmark of GR, and the decor is businesslike in discreet creams and beiges. The dishes are beautifully designed, for flavours and looks, with a dazzling choice: Pan fried Scottish sea scallops with a *millefeuille* of potato, parmesan *velouté* and truffle smarties, for instance, followed by Chargrilled monkfish tail with confit duck, layered aubergine, buttered courgettes and red wine sauce. The desserts are bliss on the tongue; try the Bitter chocolate cylinder with coffee granité and ginger mousse.

2 £££ The Capital, *Capital Hotel, 63–64 Basil Street, Tel: 020 7589 5171, open daily 12–2.30 & 6.45–10.30, Underground: Knightsbridge.* Eric Chavot, protégé of Raymond Blanc, is the genius head chef of The Capital which has been awarded 2 Michelin stars. Chavot has been here since 1999, and the restaurant has been newly refurbished in an elegant, slightly old-fashioned style. Surprisingly good combinations include Langoustine with honey-glazed pork belly, and Fricassée of frogs' legs, veal sweetbreads and cèpe purée. The separate dessert menu is a pleasure to read and the real article a delight to behold.

3 ££ Bibendum, *81 Fulham Road, Tel: 020 7581 5817, open Mon–Fri 12–2.30 & 7–11, Sat 12.30–3 & 7–11.30, Sun 12.30–3 & 7–10.30, Underground: South Kensington.* ■ A relaxed but smart place to eat, occupying the former Michelin tyre showrooms (1909–11; *pictured overleaf*). The modern Conran design

a/s/e London

Bibendum restaurant housed in the former Michelin tyre showroom on the Fulham Road

has fun with the building's origins. The restaurant with its huge stained glass windows, serves reassuringly reliable and unfussy food, both British and traditional French. Starters to sample might be Escargots de Bourgogne or Salad of smoked eel, Jersey Royals and crisp panacetta and watercress velouté. Deep-fried haddock, chips and tartare sauce or Magret de canard, with wild mushrooms, foie gras and cèpe *parmentier* might follow. Desserts include Steamed ginger pudding with custard or

Tarte fine aux pommes. On the ground floor is an Oyster Bar.

4 ££ Racine, *229 Brompton Road, Tel: 020 7584 4477, open Mon–Fri 12–3 & 6–10.30, Sat 12–3.30 & 6.30–10.30, Sun 12–3 & 6–10, Underground: South Kensington.* Close to the V&A, and not far from the French Consulate and Lycée, the Racine is reassuringly as traditional a *bistrot* as one could find. The unpretentious setting, the uncomplicated food, and the reasonable prices make this a very popular place and it is essential to book. Revel in traditional French dishes (rarely available in Paris any more) such as *soup à l'oignon*, *raclette*, or Celeriac *rémoulade*, and round it off with a *petit pot au chocolat*.

5 £ Rotisserie Jules, *6–8 Bute Street, Tel: 020 7584 0600, open Mon–Sat 12–3 & 6–10.30, Sun 12–10.30, Underground: South Kensington.* Simplicity itself combined with excellent value for money. Eat in or take away, the succulent spit roasted leg of lamb, chicken or duck, is designed to be shared. The *pommes dauphinoises* are excellent, and as well as the rotisserie, there are warm salads, soups and sandwiches, and a small wine selection.

shop

Kensington, Chelsea and Knightsbridge provide some of the most upmarket shopping in London. Knightsbridge's busy shopping street is dominated by the two mighty department stores, Harrods and Harvey Nichols. Its neighbours Sloane Street and Sloane Square are lined with haute couture and designer addresses. The stylish Duke of York Square (*map p. 121, F4–G4*) is a relaxing place with pleasant pavement cafés ready to revive you for the shopping opportunities on the King's Road. All shops are located on map pp. 120 & 121, and are generally open Mon–Sat 10–6 or 7, Sun 12–6, with late night opening on Thursdays.

KNIGHTSBRIDGE

Harrods, *87–137 Brompton Road, Tel: 020 7589 0170, Underground: Knightsbridge*. The instantly recognisable terracotta bulk of Harrods, built in 1894, is a magnet to Londoners and visitors alike. Famed worldwide as the largest luxury-goods emporium, the Daily Telegraph in 1894 carried the slogan 'Harrods serves the world'. Indeed its service is second to none and it is a world in itself. The first building in London to install escalators (1898), the wondrous Food Hall is decorated with hunting scenes, a fitting tribute to Harrods beginnings in 1849 when Henry Charles Harrod opened a modest grocer's shop (Harrods was purchased by the Al Fayed brothers in 1985 for a cool £615 million). The business was expanded by his son Charles from 1860 and now stocks just about anything you could wish for, from the most costly jewellery to best back bacon. There are acres of furniture; Vivienne Westwood, Nick Tentis and Holland Esquire claim to produce the most perfect couture outfit or tailored suit by using a Bodymetrics scan; Home and Lifestyle includes customised bedlinen and bespoke tablewear and accessories for the most pampered pet; numerous bars and restaurants serve everything from a pizza to world-class sushi; and a well-stocked beauty department offers advice and treatments. At Christmas, a fairytale grotto comes to life, and January marks the most famous of all sales when hundreds of shoppers queue outside the store ready to purchase as many bargains as they can carry home. **Map p. 121, E3**

a/s/e London

135

A Harvey Nichols, *102–125 Knightsbridge, Tel: 020 7235 5000, Underground: Knightsbridge*. Even older than Harrods (it started life in 1813 as a linen shop), Harvey Nichols is in some ways the more glamorous sister of Harrods. Familiarly known as 'Harvey Nicks', it is the showcase for sought-after designer labels such as Alexander McQueen, John Galliano and Jean-Paul Gaultier and for men, Lanvin Paris, Limoland, and Christian Audigier. Innovative lifestyle names are also stocked, including beautiful and practical Culti furniture, After Noah retro-look toys and exclusive Omorovicza skincare products.

THE KING'S ROAD

B Catimini, at no. 33c (*Tel: 020 7824 8897*), is positively *le dernier cri* in children's clothes; everything beautifully co-ordinated in vibrant colours. **C Tabio**, at no. 94 (*Tel: 020 7591 1960*), stocks socks, socks, socks: in stripes and multi-stripes, polka dots and bold colours; knee high, mid-calf, ankle or 'socketts'. **D Korres Natural Products**, at no. 124 (*Tel: 020 7581 6455*), is a beautiful shop offering a range of hair and skin care, and sun creams based on some 3,000 herbal and natural remedies. **E Mirage**, at no. 178 (*Tel: 020 7751 4520*), has elegant clothes under their own label, also Barbara Bui shoes and bags, and designs by Sylvie Schimmel. A couple of shops down, at no. 186, is **Ekyog** (*Tel: 020 7352 3255*), a French line dedicated to producing garments using 100% organic fibres and toxic-free dyes as well as having a Fair Trade label.

SLOANE SQUARE & SLOANE STREET

F Peter Jones (*Tel: 020 7730 3434*), a 1930s department store, dominates Sloane Square. With its ocean-liner inspired design, it is something of a Chelsea institution. In May it is adorned with flowers when the influence of the Chelsea Flower Show overflows onto the shopfronts of the square. **G David Mellor**, at no. 4 Sloane Square (*Tel: 020 7730 4259*), has an undisputed reputation for beautifully designed cutlery; the entire range of cutlery and kitchen utensils is an exercise in discreet perfection. Opposite, at no. 53, is **Emma Hope** (*Tel: 020 7259 9566*) selling her original footwear designs, all beautifully handcrafted in Tuscany; racy high-heeled platforms, cowboy boots and sequinned slip-ons. **H Jo Malone**, at no. 150 Sloane Street (*Tel: 020 7730 2100*), echoes the understated elegance of the black and white packaging used for her goods. Jo started in facials and has expanded into beauty products, make-up, candles and gifts. While making your choice, a complimentary arm and hand massage is offered at the Tasting Bar.

art glossary

Art Nouveau Decorative style originating in England in the 1880s, spreading through western Europe and America, in reaction to the historical imitation of much mid-nineteenth-century art. The style typically incorporates sinuous, vegetal forms and arabesques. The Victoria & Albert Museum (*see p. 128*) has an extensive collection of Art Nouveau articles.

Bacon, Francis (1909–92) Self-taught painter known for his deeply expressionistic and emotional works representing male and female figures, carcasses and dogs. Examples are in the Tate collections (*see pp. 28 & 104*).

Blake, Willaim (1757–1827) Printmaker, painter, engraver and poet, Blake was born in London and spent much of his life working in the city. A Romanticist, producing illustrations and paintings of imaginary subjects in an era when landscape and portraiture prevailed, Blake's work was largely ignored and cast aside as eccentric until well after his death. He created a new printing technique to produce poetry and illustrations together, using engraved copper plates. Due to the loyalty of a few patrons, particularly fellow painter John Linnell, he was able to carry on his innovative work without financial worries. Many of Blake's works can be viewed at the Blake Collection at Tate Britain (*see p. 103*).

Bloomsbury Group Influential group of early 20th-century artists, writers and intellectuals whose base was the house of Virginia Woolf and her sister Vanessa Bell; 46 Gordon Square, Bloomsbury (*map p. 67, A5*). Leading members included Virginia and Vanessa, the writers E.M.Forster and Lytton Strachey and the artists and critics Clive Bell, Roger Fry, Duncan Grant and Henry Lamb. The group's elitist idea that nothing mattered more in life than art and culture had a great influence on avant-garde art in Britain. Bloomsbury Group artworks can be seen at the National Portrait Gallery (*see p. 80*), the Courtauld Gallery (*see p. 85*), and Tate Britain (*see p. 104*).

Cartoon A full-scale drawing worked out in detail to transfer to a painting, tapestry or stained glass. The Raphael Cartoons at the Victoria & Albert Museum (*see p. 126*) are one of the most famous examples.

Constable, John (1776–1837) Outstanding landscape artist; one of Britain's most famous and admired, along with Turner (*see p. 142 below*). Constable spent time living and working in London but the focus for many of his most famous works, such as *Flatford Mill* (*see p. 103*) and *The Hay Wain* (*see p. 78*), was 'Constable country': the countryside on the Suffolk/Essex border where he grew up. Unlike Turner, Constable didn't achieve early success and fame in Britain; his works were more widely appreciated in France.

Flaxman, John (1755–1826) Neoclassical sculptor, much admired in both England and Europe, who brought an austerity and religious element to his work. He was best known for reliefs and monuments, of which his monument to Admiral Nelson at St Paul's Cathedral (*see p. 48*) is a wonderful example.

Foster, Sir Norman (b. 1935) One of the most acclaimed British architects of today, he founded his architectural firm Foster & Parners in 1967 which has worked on projects including the Gherkin tower, City Hall and the Great Court at the British Museum (*see p. 69*).

Futurism Art movement from the early 20th century originating in Italy celebrating the modern world, particularly technology and speed. Futurist works by artists such as Umberto Boccioni can be seen at Tate Modern (*see p. 29*).

Gainsborough, Thomas (1727–88) Britain's foremost portrait painter, along with Joshua Reynolds (*see p. 141 below*). Working outside London initially, Gainsborough moved to the capital when he became a foundation member of the Royal Academy of Arts (*see p. 110*) in 1768. Technically skilfull, elegantly executed works gained the artist many wealthy clients. The beautiful portrait of his wife is shown at the Courtauld Gallery (*see p. 85*); other works, including landscapes, can be viewed at Tate Britain (*see p. 103*).

Gibbons, Grinling (1648–1721) Woodcarver who set up a large workshop in London following the Great Fire (*see pp. 54–55*) in 1666. His work was much in demand by the Crown and Christopher Wren (*see p. 142*). The choir stalls and organ case in St Paul's Cathedral are some of his best work (*see p. 46*).

Gothic Term applied to architecture constructed mainly between the late-12th and 15th centuries. Characteristic style features are the pointed arch, ribbed vault and flying buttress. These structural elements provided the means to reduce masonry to a skeletal minimum and to achieve churches of great height. A decorative feature is the rose window. Westminster Abbey (*see p. 105*) is one of England's finest Gothic churches.

Gothic Revival The medieval-style culture connected with the Romantic movement in literature in the 1830s influenced a return to the Gothic style in architecture. Championed by John Ruskin and A.W.N. Pugin, it characterises the Houses of Parliament (*see p. 110*). The last great Victorian Gothic building was the Law Courts in the Strand (*map p. 67, B8*).

Hawksmoor, Nicholas (1661–1736) Architect and, most famously, assistant to Christopher Wren (*see p. 142 below*). His own architectural designs can be seen at Christ Church Spitalfields (*see p. 63*) and the west towers of Westminster Abbey (*see p. 105*).

Hilliard, Nicholas (1547–1619) Founder of the British school of miniature painting, and Master Painter to Elizabeth I. One of the earliest paintings at Tate Britain is Hilliard's portrait of the Queen (*see p. 101*). An extensive collection of his miniatures are in the Victoria & Albert Museum (*see p. 128*).

Hogarth, William (1697–1764) One of Britain's great painters, he began by painting small and genteel family conversation pieces but moved on to moral subjects, depicted with biting satire, such as the *Rake's Progress* (1735) displayed at Sir John Soane's Museum (*see p. 86*), and *Marriage à la Mode* at the National Gallery (*see p. 78*). His fame spread through engravings of his work which demand careful 'reading'. His own exhibitions were an important forerunner to the Summer Exhibitions at the Royal Academy of Arts (*see p. 110*).

Holbein, Hans the Younger (1497–1543) German painter considered to be the greatest portraitist of all time. Having worked chiefly in Switzerland, Holbein based himself in London from 1536 where he worked for Henry VIII. An engraved suit of armour for the king is on display at the Tower of London (*see p. 52*), and his artworks can be seen at the National Gallery (*see p. 77*) and the Victoria & Albert Museum (*see p. 124*).

Landseer, Sir Edwin (1802–73) Famed in his time for his sentimental paintings of animals, his popularity was assured by the sale of engravings of his works made by his brother. Landseer was Queen Victoria's favourite painter and was elected Associate of the Royal Academy of Arts in 1831, aged 24. His lions in Trafalgar Square (*see p. 87*) are much-loved.

Millais, Sir John Everett (1829–96) Painter and book illustrator who co-founded the Pre-Raphaelite Brotherhood (*see p. 140*). Gradually, Millais began to move away from Pre-Raphaelite ideals to more commercially successful and sentimental works such as the Pears soap *'Bubbles'*. His celebrated Pre-Raphaelite work, *Ophelia*, can be seen at Tate Britain (*see p. 103*). Other works are on display at the Guildhall Art Gallery (*see p. 54*).

Misericords Carved brackets on the underside of a choir stall which served as a support during long masses when clergy had to remain standing. They are frequently carved with amusing scenes.

Modernism Architectural style, also named 'International Modern', developed in both the USA and Europe (though separately) in the early 20th century. The movement came to prominence later in England. Characterised by the use of reinforced concrete and cubic shapes, the Southbank Centre is an example of Modernist architecture in London, with the Royal Festival Hall containing reproductions of its original Modernist interior decoration (*see pp. 31–32*).

Morris, William (1834–96) Remarkable polyglot of prodigious energy and talent, Morris was writer, poet, designer, print-maker and pioneering Socialist. He established the firm Morris & Co in 1861, with the objective of producing beautiful, hand-crafted objects that were affordable to everyone, however, ironically, the hand-made stained glass, carpets, wallpapers and furnishing fabrics became too expensive for the ordinary man. His fabric designs live on at Liberty's department store (*see p. 93*), and the Morris café room at the Victoria & Albert Museum (*see p. 128*).

Nash, John (1752–1835) Inspired town planner, Nash was the favoured architect of George IV. He designed Regent Street (*map p. 66, B3–C4*), Trafalgar Square (*see p. 87*) and began the alterations to Buckingham Palace (*see p. 99*). His career came to an end with the death of George IV in 1830.

Pre-Raphaelite Brotherhood Group of artists who formed in London in the mid-19th century, under the leadership of John Everett Millais (*see p. 139*), Dante Gabriel Rossetti and William Holman Hunt. The group was committed to producing highly detailed, brightly coloured art that came from individual creativity rather than from convention or rote (they considered Raphael's High Renaissance works to embody the restraints of academic art). Works by members of the Pre-Raphaelite Brotherhood are at Tate Britain (*see p. 103*).

Pugin, A.W.N. (1812–52) Architect and designer, convert to Roman Catholicism, and talented workaholic. Pugin was an impassioned supporter of the Gothic Revival (*see p. 139*). His work at the Houses of Parliament (*see* *p. 110*) brought him fame as did his tracts on design, and he was appointed Commissioner for Fine Arts for the Great Exhibition of 1851.

Reredos Screen of wood or stone that stands behind an altar, and is usually painted or carved.

Reynolds, Sir Joshua (1723–92) Described as the most important figure in the history of British painting, Reynolds concentrated mainly on portraits. He studied in Rome and a short visit to Venice on his way back left a pro-found effect on him. He was an enthusiastic advocate of the principle of the 'Grand Manner', created by combining an observation of nature with knowl-edge of the antique, which he set out in fifteen *Discourses* between 1769–90. After a visit to Antwerp in 1781, he adopted a more emotional approach under the influence of Rubens. He was made President of the Royal Academy of Arts at its foundation. His works can be seen at Tate Britain (*see p. 103*) and the Wallace Collection (*see p. 83*).

Rococo Art form which emerged from early 18th-century France as a pro-gression from Baroque. The name derives from the french *rocaille*, rock-work or shell-work, often used on fountains and grottoes. Mainly applied to interior decoration, it was characterised by sumptuousness, light-hearted-ness and elegance, in contrast to Baroque's darker colours and more weighty themes. Rococo paintings often depict natural settings and centre on the upper-class life and light-hearted romance, rather than religious or heroic topics. Jean-Honoré Fragonard's *The Swing*, on show at the Wallace Collection (*see p. 83*), is the very epitome of Rococo style.

Scott, Sir George Gilbert (1811–78) Prolific Victorian architect and enthusi-astic restorer. Scott was the son of a clergyman and an evangelical. He began his career building workhouses, and became surveyor of Westminster Abbey (*see p. 105*) in 1849. He went on to receive many com-missions for churches, and favoured a blend of Anglo-French High Gothic. The Albert Memorial (*see p. 130*) is one of his most successful projects and fully representative of the period.

Soane, Sir John (1753–1837) One of England's most important and original architects, superficially a Neoclassicist. He rebuilt his house at 12 Lincoln's Inn Fields in a daringly modern manner and used it to house his fascinating collection of antiquities (*see p. 86*). One of his major influences was the French Neoclassical architect Claude-Nicolas Ledoux, but he introduced a more Romantic element into his later work.

Turner, Joseph Mallord William (1775–1851) Genius painter of landscapes, born in Covent Garden, Turner was already a Royal Academician at 27. He was a master of watercolour with which he could capture the most magical effects of light. Subjects ranged from atmospheric landscapes and effects of weather, to contemporary events. He was first indebted to the Dutch landscapists but Italian influences filtered in through Claude Lorrain and his first visit to Italy in 1819. He also travelled extensively to Switzerland, Germany and France where he produced some of his most brilliant works. In advance of his time, his Romantic style was sometimes considered unfinished, and has been described as 'coloured light'. He bequeathed nearly 300 paintings and nearly 20,000 watercolours and drawings to the nation; Tate Britain has its own remarkable Turner Collection (see p. 104).

Van Dyck, Anthony (1599–1641) Pivotal in the history of English portrait painting was the Flemish artist, Anthony van Dyck, who settled in England in 1632 and introduced innovations learned from Rubens and in Italy. He enjoyed great success as Court Painter to Charles I, who awarded him a knighthood, and was particularly sought after as a portrait painter. Some of his exceptional works can be seen at the National Gallery (see p. 77) and the National Portrait Gallery (see p. 79).

Vorticism Art movement dating from 1914 and founded by the artist and writer Wyndham Lewis. Vorticist art combined the fragmented reality of Cubism with the embracing of the modern machine world of Futurism. The Vorticists held one exhibition in London in 1915 before the mechanised destruction of the First World War brought an end to the movement. Works can be seen at Tate Modern (see p. 29) and Tate Britain (see p. 104).

Wren, Sir Christopher (1632–1723) One of the most influential and innovative architects in England (see box on p. 47), he brought together his knowledge of mathematics, engineering and physics to create buildings of extraordinary originality. He began his architectural career in the 1660s and was appointed to the commission for the restoration of St Paul's Cathedral before the Great Fire (1666), and afterwards became one of the Surveyors under the Rebuilding Act. He demonstrated his genius in the masterful design for St Paul's Cathedral (see p. 44) with its beautiful and technically brilliant dome. He also supervised the rebuilding of 51 City churches (see p. 56).

index

Numbers in italics are picture references. Numbers in bold denote major references.

a/s/e London

a/s/e London

The author and the publisher have made reasonable efforts to ensure the accuracy of all the information in this book; however, they can accept no responsibility for any loss, injury or inconvenience sustained by any traveller as a result of information or advice contained in the guide.

Every effort has been made to contact the copyright owners of material reproduced in this guide. We would be pleased to hear from any copyright owners we have been unable to reach.

Statement of editorial independence: the publisher, their authors and editors, are prohibited from accepting any payment from any hotel, restaurant, gallery or other establishment for its inclusion in this guide, or for a more favourable mention than would otherwise have been made.

art/shop/eat London
Fully rewritten second edition 2008

Published by Blue Guides Limited, a Somerset Books Company
Winchester House, Deane Gate Avenue, Taunton, Somerset, TA1 2UH
www.artshopeat.com
www.blueguides.com
© Blue Guides Limited
Blue Guide is a registered trademark

ISBN 978-1-905131-25-9

Editor: Sophie Livall
Photo editor: Hadley Kincade
Layout and design: Anikó Kuzmich, Regina Rácz
Maps: Dimap Bt, reproduced by permission of Ordnance Survey
on behalf of HMSO. © Crown copyright 2008. All rights reserved.
Ordnance Survey Licence No. 100043799
Floor plans: Imre Bába
Printed in Singapore by Tien Wah Press Pte

Photo credits: p. 151, which forms part of this copyright page

We welcome all comments, corrections and views. We want to hear all
feedback, and as a mark of gratitude we will be happy to send a free copy of
one of our books to anyone providing useable corrections, constructive
criticism, or gross flattery. Please contact us via our website,
www.artshopeat.com

SOMERSET BOOKS